How to Cook

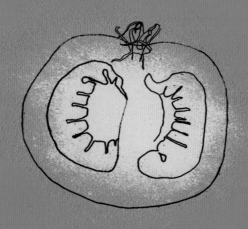

LONDON, NEW YORK, MELBOURNE, MUNICH, AND DELHI

Senior editor Francesca Baines
Senior art editor Sheila Collins
Editors Matilda Gollon, Ashwin Khurana
Designers Hoa Luc, Katie Knutton
Managing editor Linda Esposito
Managing art editor Jim Green

Category publisher Laura Buller
Design development manager Sophia M. Tampakopoulos Turner
Development team Laura Brim, Jayne Miller
Senior production controller Angela Graef
Production editor Clare McLean
DK picture library Rob Nunn
Jacket editor Matilda Gollon
Jacket designer Laura Brim

US consultant Chef Jill Lawrence
Step-by-step illustrations Maltings Partnership
Other illustrations Hennie Haworth, Rosie Scott
Original photography Dave King
Home economist for photography Katy Greenwood

First published in the United States in 2011 by
DK Publishing, 375 Hudson Street,
New York, New York 10014

08 09 10 11 12 10 9 8 7 6 5 4 3 2 1
179066—01/11

Copyright © 2011 Dorling Kindersley Limited

DK books are available at special discounts when purchased in bulk for sales promotions, premiums, fundraising, or educational use. For details, contact: DK Publishing Special Markets, 375 Hudson Street, New York, New York 10014 SpecialSales@dk.com

A CIP record for this book
is available from the Library of Congress

ISBN 978-0-7566-7214-0

High-res workflow proofed by MDP, U.K.
Printed and bound by Hung Hing, China

Discover more at
www.dk.com

How
to
Cook

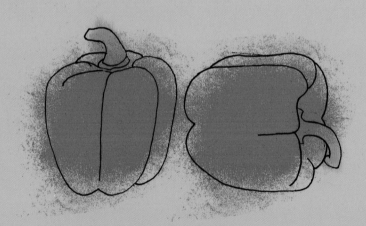

Consultant Maggie Mayhew

Contents

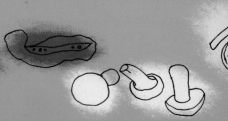

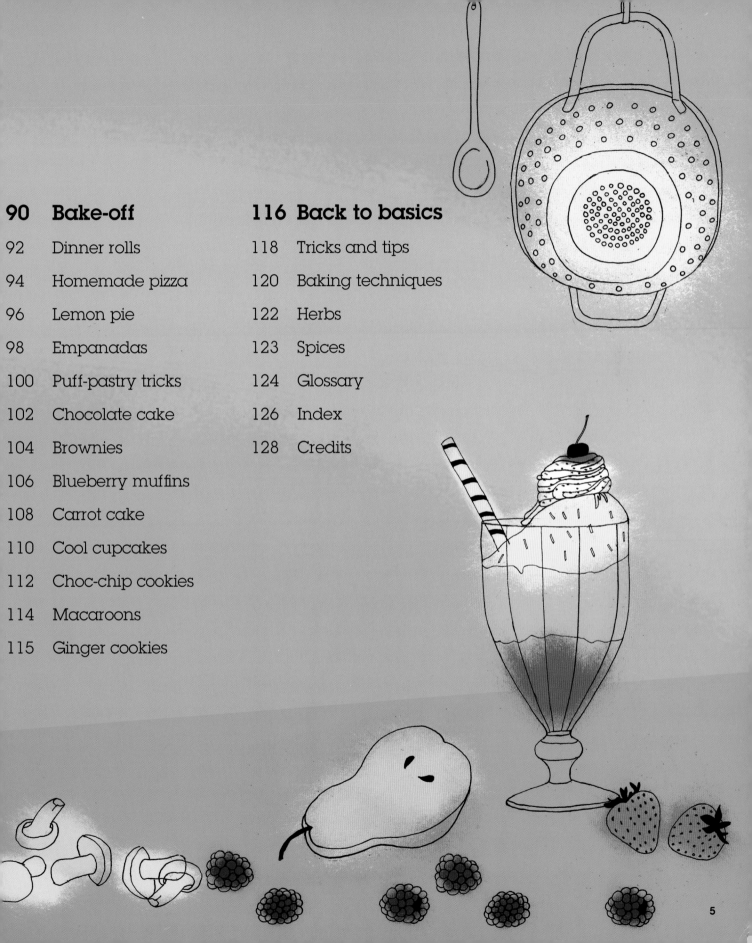

Fun with food

It's time to get cooking. Why? Because food is fun. Get a few people together, add some food, and suddenly you've got a party. It's an important part of every special occasion—birthdays, weddings, and picnics! Another good reason to learn how to cook is that it's a skill for life. You have to eat every day, so why not find out how to cook tasty dishes that you can share with your friends and family?

Confident cooking

If you haven't done it before, cooking can seem a bit daunting, so the recipes in this book explain simply and clearly how to make things. But there are also lots of tips and ideas for variations because, once you've mastered the basic techniques, we hope you'll feel confident enough to adapt recipes yourself, add in your favorite ingredients, and play around with flavors.

Healthy eating

Eating the right food is vital for good health, and every day you need to eat a variety of foods. There are five main food groups, each of which provides an important part of your diet.

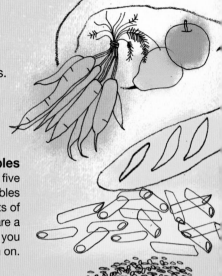

Fruit and vegetables

You should eat at least five portions of fruits and vegetables each day. They contain lots of vitamins and minerals and are a source of fiber, especially if you eat them with their skin on.

Fats and sugars

Your body needs some fat, but too much is bad for you. The best types of fats are found in oily fish (such as tuna and salmon), nuts, seeds, avocados, and oils. Sugar provides energy, but too much can lead to obesity and is bad for your teeth.

Carbohydrates

Bread, potatoes, grains, cereals, rice, and pasta give you energy. Whole-grain breads and cereals are higher in fiber and give longer-lasting energy than white bread and processed cereals.

Dairy products

Dairy foods such as milk and cheese contain calcium. Your body needs this mineral to keep your bones, teeth, nails, and hair in good repair. Skim and nonfat milk contain as much calcium as whole milk but are lower in fat.

Proteins

Protein helps you grow, builds your muscles, and keeps you strong. It is found in meat, fish, eggs, nuts, seeds, and legumes (such as dried peas, beans, and lentils).

A balanced diet

It's important to get the balance of the different foods in your diet right. This plate has been divided to show the percentage of each type of food you should aim to eat each day.

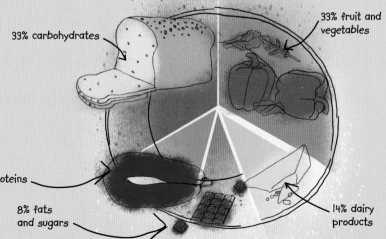

33% carbohydrates

33% fruit and vegetables

12% proteins

8% fats and sugars

14% dairy products

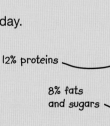

In the kitchen

Cooking involves working with heat and using equipment that must be handled with care, such as sharp knives. Common sense and the guidelines below will help you to stay safe in the kitchen, but always ask an experienced cook for help if you need it. If you are unsure of any cooking techniques, such as how to prepare a chili, or separate an egg, turn to the back of the book, where they are explained.

Hygiene

- Always wash your hands before you start.
- Wash all fruit and vegetables.
- Any chopping board or knife used in the preparation of raw poultry, meat, or fish should be cleaned thoroughly with hot soapy water before using it again.
- Raw eggs carry a risk of contamination from the salmonella bacterium. Do not give foods with uncooked eggs in them to babies and young children, pregnant women, or the elderly.
- Use separate cutting boards for meat and vegetables.
- Always check the use-by and best-before dates on ingredients and don't use them if the date has passed.

Safety

- Always use oven mitts when handling hot pots and pans.
- Don't put hot pans directly onto the work surface, but use a heat mat, metal rack or trivet, or wooden or heatproof board.
- A sharp knife is safer than a dull one, but remember that sharp knives should be used carefully and treated with respect.
- Wear an apron to protect your clothes.
- Keep the cooking area clean, and wipe up any spills that could cause accidents.

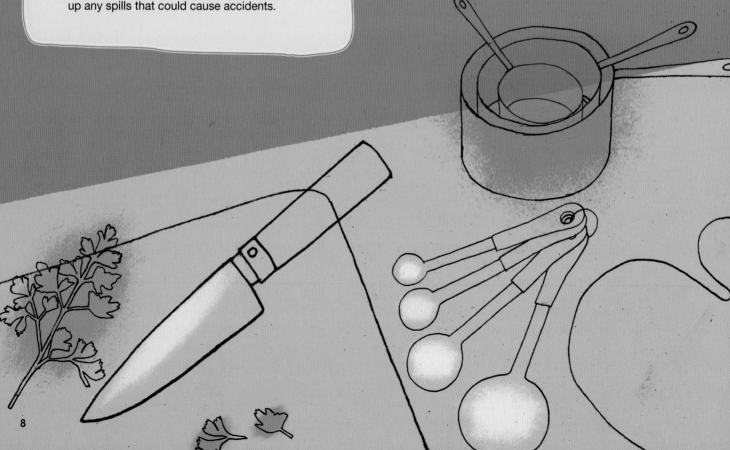

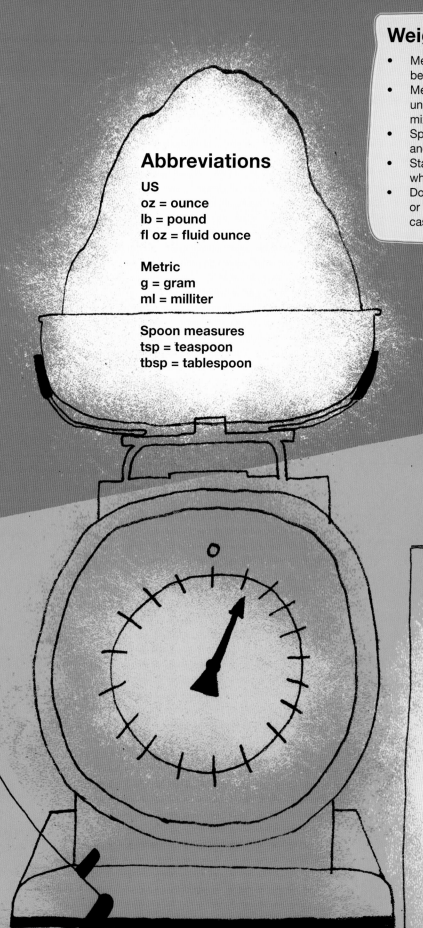

Abbreviations

US
oz = ounce
lb = pound
fl oz = fluid ounce

Metric
g = gram
ml = milliter

Spoon measures
tsp = teaspoon
tbsp = tablespoon

Weighing ingredients

- Measure and weigh all of the ingredients before you start cooking.
- Measurements are given in both US and metric units. Use either system, but don't mix them within a recipe.
- Spoons refer to measuring spoons, not flatware, and they should be level, not heaped.
- Stand a measuring cup on a flat surface when using it.
- Don't pour ingredients into measuring spoons or cups over the food you are preparing in case it spills into the mixture.

Cook's notes

- Gather and prepare all of the ingredients before you start cooking—you don't want to discover halfway through a recipe that you have run out of something important.

- All fruits and vegetables listed in recipes are medium sized unless stated otherwise.

- Use medium-sized eggs unless stated otherwise and free range if possible.

- Always use the type of flour specified in a recipe—bread, all-purpose, or self-rising.

- It's important to preheat the oven for 10 minutes or so before using it to allow for the correct temperature to be reached.

- Preparation and cooking times are only a guide. Cooking times may vary according to the type of pan, or oven, and the ripeness of ingredients.

- The easiest way to make cooking stock is using a stock cube, or bouillon powder, with the correct quantity of water, according to the instructions on the package.

Food fast

If you find yourself short on time or get home needing food fast, it doesn't mean you can't eat well or that you need to turn to junk food. There are lots of tasty snacks you can rustle up quickly, or cook ahead.

Minestrone

There is nothing quite like a hearty soup to warm the bones on a chilly winter's evening. Minestrone—which literally means "big soup"—is a delicious Italian recipe that combines fresh vegetables, pasta, and aromatic herbs.

SERVES 4
PREPARATION: 30 MINUTES
COOKING: 10 MINUTES

1 tbsp olive oil
1 onion, finely chopped
3 garlic cloves, finely chopped
2 celery ribs, finely chopped
1 large zucchini, halved
    and sliced
5½ oz (150 g) green beans,
    cut into short lengths
5 cups hot vegetable stock
2 tsp tomato paste
14 oz (400 g) can cannellini
    beans, drained
3½ oz (100 g) dried pasta, such
    as elbows or macaroni
1 tbsp pesto
salt and freshly ground
    black pepper
Parmesan cheese

1 Heat the oil in a large, deep pan over low heat. Add the onion and fry over low heat for 5 minutes, or until soft.

2 Add the garlic, celery, and zucchini. Continue to cook over low heat for 10 minutes.

3 Stir in the green beans, vegetable stock, and tomato paste, and bring to the boil. Slightly reduce the heat, then cover and simmer for about 5 minutes.

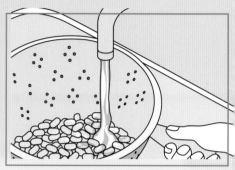

4 Rinse the cannellini beans in a colander and add them to the soup with the pasta. Bring the soup to the boil, then simmer for 10 minutes. Stir in the pesto, and season with salt and freshly ground black pepper.

5 Grate some Parmesan cheese over the soup and serve with lots of hot crusty bread.

For extra flavor, scatter fresh basil leaves or rosemary over the soup.

Beans and bacon
Try different types of beans, such as black beans or kidney beans, in place of the cannellini. You can even add some diced bacon with the onions for a meaty version.

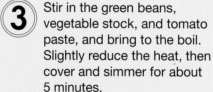

Gazpacho

This refreshing Spanish chilled soup is perfect for a hot summer's day. Gazpacho was traditionally eaten by peasants and farmers and mostly contained bread, water, and olive oil pounded together. Tomatoes were not added to the recipe until the 1700s.

Top Tip
Don't overfill the blender in step 3. If you have too much soup, pulse the mixture in two smaller batches.

SERVES 4
PREPARATION: 30 MINUTES,
  PLUS CHILLING

1 red bell pepper, deseeded and
  finely chopped
1 red onion, finely chopped
1 cucumber, finely chopped
2¼ lb (1 kg) tomatoes, skinned,
  deseeded, and finely chopped
1 tbsp chopped fresh parsley
3½ oz (100 g) day-old bread,
  preferably crusty
2 garlic cloves, chopped
4 tbsp olive oil, plus extra
  to serve
3 tbsp red wine vinegar
1¾ cups chilled water
salt and freshly ground
  black pepper

1 Put the pepper, onion, cucumber, and tomatoes in a mixing bowl with the parsley.

2 Pulse the bread in a blender with the garlic, then add it to the mixing bowl with the olive oil and vinegar. Slowly add the water to give the mixture a thick consistency.

3 Transfer the mixture from the bowl to the blender and pulse for 10 seconds. Don't worry if you can see a few chunks of cucumber, but if you prefer a smoother soup, blend for a little longer, adding extra water if the consistency is too thick.

4 Season with salt and freshly ground black pepper. Transfer the soup into a serving dish and place in the refrigerator for 2–4 hours, until completely cold. To serve, drizzle with olive oil.

If you like a little spice, try adding a few drops of Tabasco sauce to the soup before eating.

Set aside 2 tbsp of chopped vegetables before blending and serve them in the soup as a garnish.

Find out how to skin tomatoes on page 118.

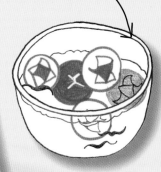

13

Simple soups

Soups are easy to make, and can be as simple or involved as you like. Enjoy them before a main course or serve them with lots of crusty bread and turn them into a meal in themselves. To add to the flavor, sprinkle over some tasty toppings, such as crispy bacon pieces or cheesy croutons. All recipes serve 4.

Grate Cheddar cheese to melt into the soup.

Pea soup
Cook 4 sliced scallions in ½ stick butter in a saucepan until soft. Add 2½ cups vegetable stock and bring to the boil. Add 3 cups frozen peas, then simmer for 3–4 minutes. Allow to cool a little, pour into a blender, then pulse until smooth. Return the soup to the saucepan and stir in ⅔ cup light cream and 2 tsp chopped fresh mint. Season with salt and freshly ground black pepper.

Small salty pieces of cooked bacon are delicious with pea soup.

Hot tortilla soup
In a pan, cook 1 chopped onion in 1 tbsp olive oil until soft with 1 garlic clove and 1 red chili, both finely chopped. Add 1 tbsp paprika, 4½ cups tomato juice, and 1¼ cups vegetable stock, and simmer for 15 minutes. Heat 4 tbsp sunflower oil in a frying pan, add 2 soft corn tortillas, cut into strips, and fry until crisp. Drain on paper towels. Stir in 2 tbsp chopped fresh cilantro and the juice of 1 lime, season with salt and freshly ground black pepper and top with tortillas.

Roasted tomato soup

Roast 12 tomatoes—about 1½ lb (675 g)—with 2 unpeeled cloves of garlic and 3 tbsp olive oil at 400°F (200°C) for about 45 minutes. When cool, squeeze the garlic out of their skins. Meanwhile, chop 1 red onion, 1 potato, and 2 ribs of celery and fry in 1 tbsp olive oil until soft. Add 4½ cups vegetable stock, 2 tsp sugar, and the roasted tomatoes and garlic. Simmer for 20 minutes. Blend until smooth, then press through a strainer.

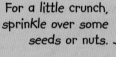

For a little crunch, sprinkle over some seeds or nuts.

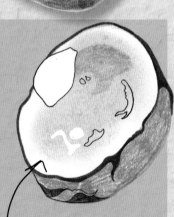

Crusty garlic bread is great for dipping in soups (see page 36).

Spicy lentil soup

Gently fry 2 onions, 2 celery ribs, and 2 carrots—all finely chopped—in 1 tbsp olive oil. Cook for 5 minutes, then add 2 finely chopped garlic cloves and 1 tsp curry powder and stir for a further 1 minute. Add ¾ cup red lentils, 6 cups vegetable stock, and ½ cup tomato juice. Bring to the boil, then turn down the heat, cover, and simmer for 25 minutes. Season with salt and freshly ground black pepper.

Cheesy croutes (large croutons) are great with soups. Cut Italian or French bread into ½ in (1 cm) slices. Toast, then rub the cut side of a halved garlic clove over one side, top with some Cheddar cheese, and broil.

Salad Niçoise

This is a great salad if you want something that's quick to make, filling, and very tasty. A specialty of the Côte d'Azur region of France and named after the city of Nice, Salad Niçoise is full of flavor, with salty anchovies and olives, juicy tuna, and fresh herbs.

SERVES 4
PREPARATION: 30 MINUTES

3 eggs
8 oz (225 g) small new
  potatoes, washed
4 oz (115 g) green beans,
  trimmed
6 small tomatoes, quartered
2 x 7 oz (200 g) can tuna in
  olive oil, drained
handful of fresh Italian
  parsley, chopped
bunch of fresh chives,
  finely chopped
12 black olives, pitted
1¾ oz (50 g) can anchovies,
  drained
1 head iceberg lettuce, leaves
  separated and washed

For the dressing
6 tbsp olive oil
2 tbsp white wine vinegar
1 garlic clove, halved
2 tsp Dijon
  mustard
salt and freshly
  ground black
  pepper

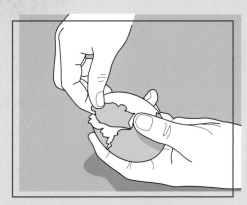

1 Cook the eggs in a pan of simmering water for about 10 minutes. Cool in cold water and then peel.

2 Boil the potatoes for about 10–15 minutes, or until tender when pierced with a knife. Drain and leave to cool, then cut in half, lengthwise. Simmer the green beans in a pan of water for 3 minutes, then drain and cool in cold water.

3 Put the potatoes, beans, tomatoes, tuna, herbs, olives, anchovies, and lettuce leaves in a large serving bowl.

4 Put all of the dressing ingredients in a screw-top jar. Season well with salt and freshly ground black pepper. Make sure the lid is on tight, then shake well to mix everything.

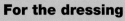

Anchovies are tiny fish preserved in salt to give them a strong, distinctive flavor. If you're not a fan, leave them out.

5 Remove the garlic from the dressing, then drizzle it over the salad and gently toss together. Quarter the eggs and arrange them on top. Serve with lots of fresh crusty bread to mop up the juices.

Assemble the salad just before you're going to eat it—if you leave the vegetables in the dressing for too long, they will lose their freshness and become soggy.

Top Tip
For a treat, use fresh tuna. Fry tuna steaks in a little olive oil for a few minutes on each side, according to how well cooked you like them, and serve on top of the salad.

Pitted olives have had their stones (pits) removed.

Cheese, please
If fish is not your thing, replace the tuna with cheese. Try slices of Greek halloumi cooked on a hot grill pan for 3 minutes on each side, or until it turns golden brown. Or use fresh mozzarella, torn into chunks, with a handful of fresh basil leaves.

Any type of tomato is good, but for a sweeter taste, try cherry tomatoes.

17

Classic salads

These salads taste fantastic and are good for you, too. Best of all, it won't take long to prepare them. Try and use really fresh ingredients, which will have more flavor. Feel free to make up your own salads, too—even a simple mix of crunchy green salad leaves is delicious with a tasty homemade dressing.

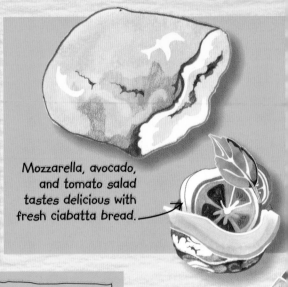

Mozzarella, avocado, and tomato salad tastes delicious with fresh ciabatta bread.

Mozzarella, avocado, and tomato salad (serves 4)

Slice 6 tomatoes, 2 peeled avocados, and 3 4½-oz (125-g) balls buffalo mozzarella and layer onto a plate. Scatter fresh basil leaves over the salad, followed by a sprinkle of salt and plenty of freshly ground black pepper. To serve, drizzle some extra virgin olive oil on top.

Leave the stalk end intact to hold the onion together while you slice the rings.

To serve, sprinkle over a handful of chopped parsley and a few oregano leaves.

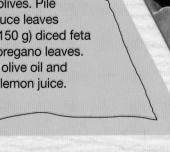

Greek salad (serves 4)

Chop 4 tomatoes into wedges and mix in a bowl with ½ a sliced cucumber, ½ a sliced red onion, 1 sliced yellow bell pepper, and a handful of black olives. Pile on top of some lettuce leaves and top with 5 oz (150 g) diced feta cheese and a few oregano leaves. Drizzle over 4 tbsp olive oil and a squeeze of fresh lemon juice.

Potato salad (serves 6)

Cook 2¾ lb (1¼ kg) new potatoes in boiling water for 15–20 minutes, or until tender when pierced with a sharp knife. Drain and allow to cool. Mix 4 tbsp mayonnaise with 2 tbsp sour cream and 2 tbsp chopped fresh chives in a large bowl. When the potatoes are cool, cut them into bite-size pieces. Stir into the mayonnaise mixture.

Season with generous amounts of freshly ground black pepper.

Honey mustard dressing

Spoon 2 tsp wholegrain mustard and 2 tsp honey into a jar, and add a pinch of salt and freshly ground black pepper, ½ finely chopped garlic clove, and 2 tbsp lemon juice. Add 6 tbsp olive oil, screw on the lid tightly, and shake.

This dressing will give your salad a sharp and sweet flavor.

French dressing

Add 2 tbsp white wine vinegar and 2 tsp Dijon mustard to a small jar and shake until well combined. Take off the lid and pour in 6 tbsp extra virgin olive oil and season with salt and plenty of freshly ground black pepper. Put the lid back on the jar and shake well.

Use the largest holes on the grater.

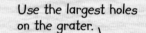

Coleslaw (serves 6)

To make the dressing, mix 3 tbsp natural yogurt with 2 tsp Dijon mustard and 3 tbsp mayonnaise. Finely slice ½ a green cabbage, grate 2 large carrots, and mix with ½ a sliced onion. Place all of the vegetables into a large bowl, and stir through the dressing. Season to taste with freshly ground black pepper.

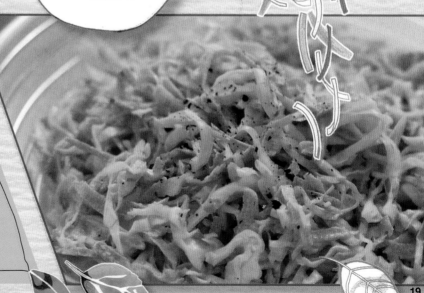

Spanish omelet

In Spain, this simple potato omelet is called *tortilla española*. The Spanish eat it all the time, as a snack, in a sandwich, and as tapas—a light meal made up of many small, tasty dishes.

Top Tip
Instead of turning the omelet over in step 4, place the pan under a broiler on medium-low heat for 5–10 minutes, or until cooked.

SERVES 4
PREPARATION: 30 MINUTES
COOKING: 25–30 MINUTES

7 fl oz (200 ml) olive oil
6 potatoes, about 2¼ lb (1 kg),
  peeled and thinly sliced
5 eggs
salt and freshly ground
  black pepper

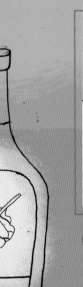

1 Heat the olive oil in a deep-sided nonstick frying pan and add the potatoes. Cook over low heat for 15 minutes, or until the potatoes are soft, stirring occasionally so that they cook evenly. Turn off the heat and leave the potatoes to cool.

2 In a large bowl, beat the eggs and plenty of seasoning with a fork. Add the potatoes with a slotted spoon in order to remove any excess oil. Stir very gently so that all of the potatoes get coated in the egg mixture, trying not to break them up too much.

3 Heat 1 tbsp of the saved olive oil in a 9-in (23-cm) frying pan and pour in the potato mixture. Reduce the heat to medium low and cook for 20 minutes, or until the bottom of the omelet is cooked.

4 Remove from the heat and slide the omelet onto a plate, and then place another plate on top. Gripping them firmly, quickly turn the plates over so that the uncooked side is now on the bottom. Slide the omelet back into the pan and cook for about 5–10 minutes, or until cooked through and golden.

5 Allow the omelet to cool in the pan for 5 minutes, then slide it out onto a plate. Leave to cool slightly for another few minutes, then slice into wedges. Serve with a salad for a snack or in a sandwich of crusty bread.

20

A Spanish omelet is delicious served cold and is great for picnics.

Add some extras

If you want some variation, try adding finely chopped onions, chopped bell peppers, sliced mushrooms, or diced chorizo to the mixture in step 1.

Easy eggs

If you've got some eggs in the fridge, there are lots of quick, tasty snacks you can make for a big breakfast, a light lunch, or a simple meal any time of the day. The ideas below are easy to prepare, delicious, and nutritious, so get cracking! All recipes serve 2.

For a sweeter French toast, use slices of panettone (a type of bread from Italy, pictured) or brioche instead of plain bread, and leave out the salt. Serve with fresh berries and a sprinkle of confectioners' sugar, or try with any type of jelly.

French toast

Whisk 2 eggs with a pinch of salt, then pour into a dish. Add 2 thick slices of bread, leave to soak, and turn over so that both sides are coated and all of the egg has soaked in. Heat a pat of butter in a frying pan. Cook the bread in the pan. When golden underneath, flip over and cook the other side. Serve sweet with maple syrup and fruit or with crispy bacon.

Snip a few fresh chives onto the eggs for a finishing touch.

Smoked salmon and scrambled eggs

Whisk 4 eggs with 2 tbsp milk and some salt and freshly ground black pepper. Melt 1 tbsp butter in a nonstick saucepan over a low heat. Pour in the eggs and stir slowly. When the mixture has formed soft lumps, turn off the heat. The eggs will continue to cook, so slightly undercook them. Butter some toasted bread or bagels and spoon the eggs on top. Top with slices of smoked salmon.

Pipérade

In a frying pan, cook 2 chopped red bell peppers with 1 sliced onion and 1 finely chopped clove of garlic in 2 tbsp olive oil over medium heat for about 20 minutes, or until very soft. Add 2 deseeded, chopped tomatoes and 1 tbsp chopped fresh parsley. Cook until the mixture becomes mushy. Season with 1 tsp sugar and some salt and black pepper. Stir in 5 whisked eggs until they start to form soft lumps. This is delicious with hot buttered toast.

To deseed a bell pepper, cut it in half through the stalk. Use a small sharp knife to cut around the stalk, core, and seeds, then discard them. Scrape out any remaining white pith and seeds.

Huevos rancheros

This is a classic Mexican breakfast—its name means "ranch eggs." Finely chop 1 onion, 1 red bell pepper, 1 garlic clove, and 1 red chili and cook with ½ tsp fresh or dried oregano in a frying pan with a little olive oil. Cook for 10 minutes, then add a 14 oz (400 g) can chopped tomatoes, some seasoning, and 1 tsp paprika, and continue to cook for a further 5 minutes. Make 4 hollows in the mixture and break an egg into each. Cover and cook for 3–5 minutes, or until the eggs are cooked. Serve with warm flour or corn tortillas.

For a meaty version, fry some sliced chorizo in the oil before adding the vegetables. It will give the dish a delicious smoky flavor.

Potato rösti

This classic dish is made from grated potatoes that are fried until crisp. You can make a big pan-sized rösti, but these smaller pancakes are easier to turn. Eat them for breakfast, or as a side dish to a main meal.

Top Tip
For some variety, try adding some extra ingredients to the potatoes, such as bacon, onion, cheese, or herbs.

MAKES 8 RÖSTI
PREPARATION: 20 MINUTES, PLUS COOLING
COOKING: 10–20 MINUTES

3–4 medium-size floury potatoes, about 1¾ lb (800 g), peeled
salt and freshly ground black pepper
4 tbsp olive oil

1 Cut the potatoes in half and parboil them in a saucepan of boiling salted water for 6–7 minutes. Drain and allow to cool.

2 Coarsely grate the potatoes into a bowl—graters with big holes are best.

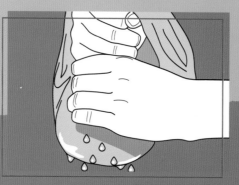

3 Use a clean dishcloth to squeeze out any excess liquid, which would make the rösti soggy. Add the salt and pepper and mix lightly with a fork.

4 Heat half of the oil in a large frying pan and let it begin to sizzle. Shape spoonfuls of the grated potato mixture into round cakes ½–¾ in (1–2 cm) thick and place four cakes into the pan.

5 Gently fry the rösti for about 5–10 minutes, or until golden brown and crisp underneath. Turn them with a spatula, then cook for a further 5–10 minutes, or until browned on the other side. Drain on paper towels and keep warm while cooking the rest of the mixture in the remaining oil.

One of the best ways to serve rösti is with a fried egg on top.

Mix your veggies

Get inventive and mix the potatoes with some other delicious root vegetables, such as sweet potatoes, carrots, parsnips, or even red beets.

Crepes

Pancakes come in all shapes and sizes and are eaten in almost every country in the world. In France people make thin pancakes called *crêpes*, which can be sweet or salty.

Top Tip
If you put in too little batter to begin with, pour in a little extra batter to fill in the gaps to cover the bottom of the pan.

MAKES 8 CREPES
PREPARATION: 10 MINUTES
COOKING: 20 MINUTES

1 cup plus 2 tbsp all-purpose
  flour
1 tsp sugar
pinch of salt
2 eggs
1¼ cups milk
2 tbsp melted butter,
  plus extra for frying

1 Sift the flour into a large bowl and add the sugar and salt. Set aside. In a separate bowl, whisk together the eggs and milk.

2 Make a well in the center of the flour mixture and gradually pour in the egg mixture, beating well until smooth, then stir in the melted butter.

3 Heat a nonstick frying pan over medium-high heat, and add a little melted butter. Ladle some of the batter into the pan, then tip the pan to spread the batter over the bottom.

4 Cook for 1–2 minutes, or until golden, then flip over with a spatula and cook for another 30 seconds. Set aside on a plate. Repeat until all of the batter is used up.

Before rolling, squeeze over some lemon juice and a sprinkle of superfine sugar.

Ham and cheese crepes
Lay a slice of ham on each crepe, sprinkle with grated cheese, and roll up. Place the crepes in a buttered frying pan and cook for 1 minute on each side, pressing down on them with a spatula so that the cheese melts.

Pancakes

Sometimes called hotcakes or flapjacks, these small, puffy pancakes are perfect for breakfast. Eat them with butter or smothered with maple syrup and fresh berries.

Top Tip
For fruity pancakes, add a large handful of fresh blueberries, raspberries, or sliced bananas to the batter before cooking and serve with vanilla ice cream.

MAKES 6 PANCAKES
PREPARATION: 10 MINUTES
COOKING: 20 MINUTES

- 1 cup plus 3 tbsp all-purpose flour
- 1 tsp baking powder
- ½ tsp salt
- 2 tbsp superfine sugar
- ½ cup milk
- 1 egg
- 2 tbsp melted butter, plus extra for frying

Stack the pancakes and drench them with maple syrup or honey. Serve with fresh strawberries, blueberries, and raspberries.

1 Sift the flour, baking powder, salt, and superfine sugar into a large bowl. Lightly beat together the milk and egg in another bowl, then whisk in the melted butter.

2 Pour the milk mixture into the flour mixture and, using a whisk, beat until smooth and all of the lumps have disappeared. Let the batter rest for a few minutes.

3 Heat a nonstick frying pan over medium heat and add a little butter. Add a spoonful of batter to the pan, or as many pancakes as you can fit, depending on the size of the pan.

4 Cook the pancakes until the tops begin to bubble and they are golden underneath. Flip them over and cook until golden brown on both sides and each pancake has risen to about ½ in (1 cm) thick.

5 Repeat until all of the batter is used up. For a real treat, serve with maple syrup and a mixture of berries.

Maple syrup is made from the sap of maple trees.

Falafel

These chickpea patties are a popular Middle Eastern snack. Spicy and delicious, falafel are great for serving up to both vegetarians and nonvegetarians. Full of protein and fiber, they're good for you, too.

MAKES 12 FALAFEL
PREPARATION: 20 MINUTES
COOKING: 6 MINUTES

14 oz (400 g) can chickpeas,
  drained
½ small onion, chopped
1 garlic clove, chopped
2 tbsp all-purpose flour
1 tsp ground cumin
1 tsp ground coriander
1 tbsp chopped fresh parsley
salt and freshly ground
  black pepper
7 fl oz (200 ml) sunflower oil

1 Place the chickpeas, onion, garlic, flour, cumin, coriander, parsley, and salt and pepper into a food processor. Blend until smooth.

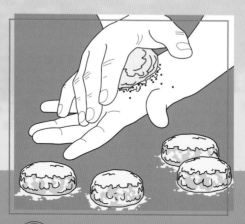

2 Lightly sprinkle the work surface with some flour and tip out the mixture from the food processor. Divide it into 12 equal portions and shape each one into a flat, round patty.

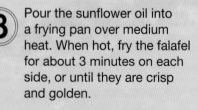

3 Pour the sunflower oil into a frying pan over medium heat. When hot, fry the falafel for about 3 minutes on each side, or until they are crisp and golden.

4 Using a spatula, carefully take out the cooked falafel and place them on a plate lined with paper towels to drain any excess oil. Serve warm or cold with a salad.

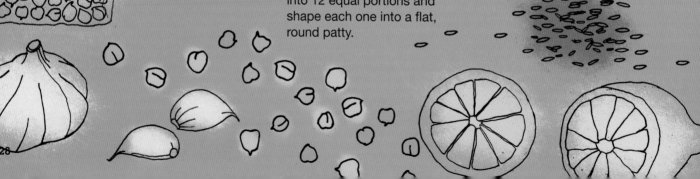

For a little extra zing, squeeze over some lemon juice just before serving.

Top Tip
If you don't have a food processor, use a potato masher or hand-held blender to break up the chickpeas in step 1 and blend them with the other ingredients.

A pita is an Arabic flatbread that puffs up when it's cooked and then collapses as it cools, creating a "pocket" in the middle that you can open up and fill.

Slice the cucumbers and finely shred the lettuce so that you can pack a lot inside the pita bread.

Packed pitas
A great way to eat falafel is packed inside pockets of pita bread. Warm a pita under the broiler, in a toaster, or in the microwave. Slice open, spread a layer of hummus (see page 31) inside, and place some falafel on top. Add some chopped salad vegetables, such as cucumbers, tomatoes, lettuce, or scallions, and a few dollops of tzatziki (see page 30).

Dips and dippers

Here are some super-quick recipes to make when you want something tasty to snack on while you're waiting for the main meal, for friends to arrive, or for the grill to get hot. Mix and match these healthy snacks as much as you like . . . just don't forget to leave some room for the main course! All recipes serve 6.

Potato wedges

Heat the oven to 425°F (220°C). Scrub some large potatoes, pat dry, cut into halves lengthwise, and then each half into three pieces. Cook the potatoes in boiling salted water for 5 minutes, then drain. Place in a baking pan and drizzle with 2 tbsp olive oil, then mix with salt, pepper, and 1 tsp paprika until coated. Bake for about 45 minutes, occasionally shaking the pan, until golden.

There's no need to peel the potatoes— the crispy skins are the best part.

Guacamole

Use a fork to mash the flesh of 2 ripe, avocados with the juice of 1 lime. Stir in ½ a chopped onion, 2 chopped tomatoes, 1 deseeded and finely chopped red chili, and 2 tbsp chopped fresh cilantro Season with salt and freshly ground black pepper.

Use only ripe avocados. To check, hold one in the palm of your hand and squeeze gently—it should give slightly.

Tzatziki

Grate ½ a peeled cucumber, sprinkle with a little salt, and squeeze in a paper towel to remove excess water. Put the grated cucumber in a bowl and mix in 1 finely chopped garlic clove, 1 cup Greek yogurt, the juice of ½ a lemon, 1 tbsp olive oil, and 1 tbsp chopped fresh mint.

Drain as much water as you can from the cucumber or the tzatziki will be very soupy.

Hummus

Drain and rinse a 14 oz (400 g) can of chickpeas and put them into a food processor. Add 2 finely chopped garlic cloves, the juice of 1 lemon, 2 tbsp tahini, 3 tbsp olive oil, and a pinch of paprika. Blend until smooth. Serve garnished with a drizzle of olive oil, a dusting of paprika, a few chickpeas, and some chopped fresh cilantro.

Vegetable sticks

Chop a colourful selection of raw salad vegetables into chunky sticks or strips and use them for dipping—carrots, red, yellow, or orange bell peppers, celery, and cucumbers are all good. They're fresh, crunchy, and healthy, too.

Bread sticks are great for dipping—look out for packages of Italian grissini, which you can keep in the pantry.

Salsa

Mix 6 chopped tomatoes, ½ a chopped onion, 1 finely chopped garlic clove, the juice of ½ a lime, 1 finely chopped and deseeded small green chili, 2 tbsp olive oil, and 2 tbsp chopped fresh cilantro. Season with salt and freshly ground black pepper.

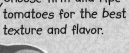

Choose firm and ripe tomatoes for the best texture and flavor.

Slice quesadillas into wedges and eat them while they're warm and the cheese is still soft and melted.

Love onions?

Make a delicious vegetarian quesadilla by leaving out the chicken, slicing an onion, and cooking it with the bell pepper in step 2.

Chicken quesadillas

Queso is Spanish for "cheese," and a quesadilla is really a Mexican version of a grilled cheese sandwich using tortillas—flatbreads made of corn or wheat flour. You can buy prepared tortillas in supermarkets. Make sure you buy soft tortillas, not tacos, which are hard. This recipe adds chicken to the mix.

MAKES 2
PREPARATION: 20 MINUTES
COOKING: 2 MINUTES

tbsp olive oil
skinned boneless chicken breast, sliced
red or yellow bell pepper, deseeded and sliced
scallions, sliced
salt and freshly ground black pepper
soft flour or corn tortillas
handful of fresh cilantro, chopped
½ oz (100 g) mild Cheddar or Monterey Jack cheese, grated

1 Heat 1 tbsp olive oil in a frying pan. Add the chicken slices and cook for 5 minutes, or until beginning to brown.

2 Add the sliced bell pepper and a pinch of salt to the chicken. Cook for 5 minutes, or until soft. Transfer the mixture to a bowl with the scallions and some freshly ground black pepper.

3 Heat the remaining oil in the frying pan and then add one tortilla. Top with half of the chicken mixture, leaving a little bit of room around the edges. Sprinkle over half of the cilantro and half of the cheese.

4 Top with another tortilla, pressing it down with the back of a spatula to sandwich the two together. After cooking for about 1 minute and when golden underneath, scoop the quesadilla up on a large spatula and carefully turn it over.

5 Cook the other side for about 1 minute, or until golden and the cheese has melted. Place on a cutting board, then repeat with the remaining ingredients. Slice both into wedges, and serve hot.

Top Tip
Guacamole and salsa (see pages 30–31) are both delicious with quesadillas. Either spread them on the tortilla in step 3, before you add the chicken, or just dollop on top.

Samosas

These spicy savoury pastries are from India, where they are usually served with chutney. Traditionally, samosas are fried, but in this healthier recipe they are baked. You can buy phyllo pastry ready-made and frozen.

MAKES 12 SAMOSAS
PREPARATION: 1 HOUR
COOKING: 20–25 MINUTES

4 potatoes, about 1 lb 5 oz (600 g), peeled and cut into large chunks

2 tbsp sunflower oil

1 tsp finely grated fresh ginger

1 garlic clove, finely chopped

1 onion, finely chopped

1 small carrot, finely chopped

3½ oz (100 g) frozen peas

1 tbsp garam masala

2 tsp cumin seeds

salt and freshly ground black pepper

2 tbsp chopped fresh cilantro

6 sheets phyllo pastry

2 tbsp melted butter, for brushing

1 Cook the potatoes in boiling salted water for 20 minutes. Drain and cool, then cut into ¼-in (5-mm) pieces. Heat the oil in a frying pan and cook the ginger, garlic, onion, and carrot for about 3 minutes, stirring until softened.

2 To the pan, add the peas, garam masala, cumin seeds, and 1 tbsp water. Season with salt and pepper and stir well. Cook for about 2 minutes, then add the diced potatoes. Continue to cook for 2 minutes, then stir in the cilantro. Set aside to cool.

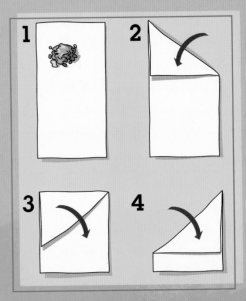

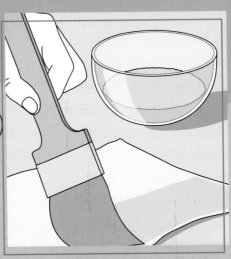

3 Preheat the oven to 400°F (200°C). Unroll the phyllo pastry, peel off one sheet, lay it flat on a clean surface, and brush with melted butter. Cut the phyllo into strips roughly 5 x 16 in (12 x 40 cm).

4 Place 1–2 tsp of the filling on one end of a strip (1). Fold a corner of the pastry over the filling to make a triangle (2). Fold down the triangle (3) and continue down the strip, alternating diagonal and straight folds, until you reach the bottom (4). Fold up any extra bits to give neat triangular parcels.

5 Place the samosas on a buttered cookie sheet, brush the tops with butter, and bake for 20–25 minutes, or until golden brown. Serve with an Indian chutney, such as mango or eggplant, or with your own homemade salsa or tzatziki (see pages 30–31).

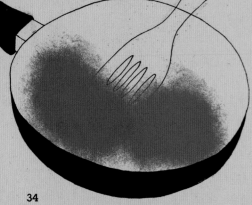

To reheat the *samosas*, put them in the oven for about 10 minutes at 400°F (200°C), or warm them in a microwave on high for 1 minute.

Make some fresh mint raita (*see* page 45) to dip the samosas in.

If you like a little spice, serve some eggplant chutney.

Meaty fillings

For a meat alternative, replace the potatoes with ground chicken or lamb. Put in about 1¼ cups ground meat at the beginning of step 2 and stir well. Cook for 5 minutes, or until browned. Continue steps 2–5 in the same way.

For a quick dip, ketchup is always popular.

Bread snacks

When you need food in a hurry, you probably turn to bread for a quick sandwich fix, using the same old fillings. But bread doesn't have to be boring—here are a few ideas to liven things up. And if you are looking for an appetizer, or something to make a soup more substantial, flavor slices of bread with garlic, tomato, and fresh herbs.

Garlic bread (serves 4)

Preheat the oven to 400°F (200°C). Mix 1 stick butter with 3 finely chopped garlic cloves, 1 tbsp chopped fresh parsley, a squeeze of lemon juice, and some seasoning. Make cuts in a baguette, without cutting all the way through. Spread the garlic butter between the slices, then wrap in foil and bake for 10 minutes.

If chopping garlic is a chore, use a crusher instead.

Crostini are a delicious appetizer.

Tomato and basil crostini (makes 12)

Cut a baguette into 12 thin slices and toast them on both sides. Mix 8 deseeded and chopped tomatoes with ½ a chopped red onion, a handful of chopped fresh basil leaves, 1 tsp balsamic vinegar and some salt. Rub each slice with a cut garlic clove, then spoon some tomato mixture on each one with a fresh basil leaf and some freshly ground black pepper. Drizzle over some olive oil before serving.

Croque monsieur (makes 4)

Make a cheesy sauce: melt 2 tbsp butter in a saucepan, stir in 2 tbsp all-purpose flour, cook for 1 minute, then remove from the heat and stir in 3½ fl oz (100 ml) milk until smooth. Beat in 2½ oz (75 g) grated Gruyère cheese, 2 tsp Dijon mustard, and 1 egg yolk. Toast 4 bread slices on one side and top each with 1 slice of ham and 1 slice of Gruyère cheese. Top with another slice of bread and spread each with a quarter of the sauce. Broil until golden.

Chicken club sandwich (makes 1)

Toast 3 slices of bread, and then spread the first slice with mayonnaise and some wholegrain mustard. Slice a small cooked, skinless chicken breast, and lay half of it, on the toast followed by 2 slices of cooked bacon. Add some sliced tomato and shredded lettuce. Top with the second slice of toast and repeat the layers. Top with the last slice of toast, secure the monster sandwich with 2 toothpicks pushed through a cornichon, cut diagonally, and enjoy!

Go vegetarian by swapping the chicken with slices of Swiss or Cheddar cheese and using watercress instead of lettuce.

Chicken Caesar wrap (makes 4)

In a blender, pulse 2 chopped anchovies with 1 finely chopped garlic clove, a squeeze of lemon juice, 2 tsp Dijon mustard, and 4 tbsp mayonnaise. Slice 4 small cooked chicken breasts and toss into the dressing. Divide the mixture between 4 soft wraps. Top with shredded lettuce, grated carrot, fresh grated Parmesan cheese, and freshly ground black pepper and roll up.

For a veggie wrap, leave out the anchovies from the dressing and fill the soft wraps with sliced avocado, cucumber sticks, and grilled red bell peppers. Top with lettuce, Parmesan cheese, and the dressing before rolling.

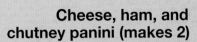

Cheese, ham, and chutney panini (makes 2)

Cut 2 panini or ciabatta rolls in half and fill each with 1¾ oz (50 g) thin sliced smoked ham, 1 tbsp chutney, and 1 slice of Cheddar or Swiss cheese. Brush the tops with olive oil, and cook on a hot grill pan, pressing down well and turning until golden on both sides and the cheese is melted.

Toast the panini in a grill pan—but if you don't have one, a regular frying pan is fine.

Big food

Everyone needs to eat one main meal each day to keep them going, so learn how to cook what you like to eat—a warming stew, a big plate of pasta, or a spicy stir-fry. Be sure to make enough. Hungry people appear from nowhere when there are tempting smells and the sounds of activity from the kitchen!

Snip some scallions and parsley leaves on top for flavor and color.

Pot of veggies

For a vegetarian jambalaya, skip to step 2 and fry the ingredients in 1 tbsp sunflower oil. Add 1 diced sweet potato or butternut squash, 1 cup frozen peas, and 1 drained 14 oz (400 g) can of kidney beans. Follow the rest of the recipe until the vegetables are cooked.

Jambalaya

This colorful one-pan rice dish is full of the flavors of the Cajun cooking from Louisiana. Its name literally means "jumbled" or "mixed up" because it is a mix of rice, meat, seafood, and vegetables.

Top Tip
You can use cooked shrimp, too—just stir them in at the very end of the recipe for 1 minute, or until heated through.

SERVES 6
PREPARATION: 30 MINUTES
COOKING: 25 MINUTES

7 oz (200 g) chorizo or any other spicy sausage, sliced

2 skinless chicken breasts, cut into bite-size pieces

1 onion, finely chopped

2 garlic cloves, finely chopped

1 red bell pepper, deseeded and chopped

2 celery ribs, diced

1 green chili, deseeded and finely chopped

1½ cups long-grain rice

1 tsp chili powder

2 tbsp tomato paste

2 tsp dried thyme

½ tsp paprika

salt and freshly ground black pepper

14 oz (400 g) can chopped tomatoes

3¾ cups vegetable stock

7 oz (200 g) raw peeled shrimp

Leave the chili seeds in if you like a little heat!

1 In a large frying pan dry fry the chorizo for 2 minutes over medium heat until it releases its golden oil. Add the chicken and fry for 3–4 minutes until browned. Remove the chorizo and chicken and set aside.

3 Return the chorizo and chicken to the pan and add the thyme, and paprika and season with salt and pepper. Pour in the tomatoes and the stock, stir, then bring to the boil.

4 Reduce the heat to low, cover tightly with a lid or foil, and simmer for 20 minutes, stirring occasionally. Stir in the shrimp and cook for a further 5 minutes, or until the liquid has been absorbed, the rice is tender, and the shrimp are pink.

2 Add the onion, garlic, bell pepper, celery, and green chili to the pan and fry, stirring, for 5 minutes, or until softened. Add the rice, chili powder, and tomato paste and cook for 2 minutes.

Chicken jalfrezi

Curry recipes can look a little daunting, but don't be put off by the long list of ingredients—most are small quantities of spices. This dish is very simple to make and has a rich tomato sauce.

Top Tip
You can adjust the heat by varying the type of chili you use. Small, thin, and round ones are usually hotter, but just use one large fat one if you prefer a milder curry.

SERVES 4
PREPARATION: 25 MINUTES
COOKING: 15 MINUTES

1 tbsp sunflower oil
1-in (2.5-cm) piece fresh
  ginger, peeled and
  finely chopped
3 garlic cloves, finely chopped
1 onion, sliced
2 tsp ground cumin
2 tsp black mustard seeds
1 tsp ground turmeric
2 tbsp masala curry paste
1 red bell pepper, deseeded
  and sliced
½ green bell pepper, deseeded
  and sliced
2 green chilies, deseeded
  and sliced
1½ lb (675 g) skinless
  chicken breast, diced
14 oz (400 g) can
  chopped tomatoes
3 tbsp chopped fresh cilantro
salt and freshly ground
  black pepper

1 Heat the oil in a large saucepan over medium heat. Add the ginger, garlic, and onion and fry until the onion starts to soften. Stir in the spices and curry paste and cook for a further 1–2 minutes.

2 Add the bell peppers and chilies and fry for 5 minutes. Turn up the heat, add the chicken, and cook for 5 minutes, or until lightly browned.

3 Add the tomatoes and cilantro. Season with salt and pepper, then reduce the heat and simmer for 15 minutes, or until the sauce has reduced slightly. Serve with plain rice or any of the side dishes on pages 44–45.

Chickpea curry

As with most spicy dishes, the flavors of this vegetarian curry are often better the next day, so look forward to any leftovers—if there are any!

Top Tip
You can swap the butternut squash with the same quantity of pumpkin, sweet potatoes, or even plain potatoes.

SERVES 4
PREPARATION: 15 MINUTES
COOKING: 20–25 MINUTES

2 tbsp sunflower oil

1 onion, finely chopped

2 garlic cloves, finely chopped

1-in (2.5-cm) piece fresh ginger, peeled and finely chopped

1 green chili, deseeded and finely chopped

1 tsp ground cumin

1 tsp ground coriander seed

1 tsp ground turmeric

1 butternut squash, about 1 lb 10 oz (750 g), peeled, seeds scooped out, and diced

14 oz (400 g) can chopped tomatoes

14 oz (400 g) can coconut milk

14 oz (400 g) can chickpeas, drained

7 oz (200 g) fresh spinach, chopped

handful of fresh cilantro, chopped

½ lemon

1 Heat the oil in a large pan over medium heat and fry the onion, garlic, ginger, and chili with the spices for about 5 minutes, until the onion starts to soften. Add the butternut squash and mix with the ingredients in the pan.

2 Pour in the tomatoes, coconut milk, and chickpeas and simmer for 15–20 minutes, or until the squash is tender when you pierce it with a fork.

3 Stir in the spinach, and when it has wilted, add the cilantro and a squeeze of lemon juice. Serve with plain rice or any of the side dishes on pages 44–45.

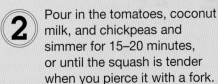

Use low-fat coconut milk for a healthier version.

Curry feast

It's fun and traditional to serve Indian curries with a selection of side dishes, including breads, relishes, vegetables, and flavored rice. Here are some delicious dishes—pick one or two to eat with a curry or make them all for a real Indian feast! All recipes serve 4–6.

Naan breads are great for mopping up curry sauces. Buy them at the supermarket and follow the instructions on the package to heat them up in the oven.

Indian salad
Mix together 1 finely chopped red onion, 1 deseeded and finely chopped green chili, 2 finely chopped tomatoes, finely chopped ¼ of a cucumber, a small handful of chopped fresh mint, and a handful of chopped fresh cilantro. Season with salt and freshly ground black pepper, then cover and chill until ready to serve.

Top the dahl with some extra fried onions and chilies.

Dahl
Cook 1 chopped onion in 3 tbsp sunflower oil until soft. Stir in 1 cinnamon stick, a 1¼-in (3-cm) piece grated fresh ginger, 1 tsp each of ground turmeric, ground cumin, and ground coriander seed, and 1 cup split red lentils. Add 3 cups vegetable stock and 1 bay leaf. Season, then simmer for 25–30 minutes, stirring frequently, until soft and mushy. Fry 3 sliced garlic cloves and 1 deseeded and chopped red chili in 2 tbsp sunflower oil until golden. Stir into the lentils with 2 tbsp fresh lemon juice and serve.

Raita
Coarsely grate ½ a peeled and deseeded cucumber onto paper towels and squeeze out the excess water. Stir into 1 cup natural yogurt with a small handful of chopped fresh mint, a pinch of salt, and 1 tsp of superfine sugar.

For a spicy kick, add ½ tsp ground cumin to the raita.

Popadoms are thin, crispy flatbreads made from gram flour. Buy them already prepared, and dip them in chutney or raita—or top with Indian salad.

Stir in ¾ cup thawed frozen peas to the pilaf for color.

Spicy rice pilaf
Heat 1 tbsp sunflower oil in a large saucepan. Add 1 small finely chopped onion and fry until golden. Stir in 1 cinnamon stick, 1 tsp cumin seeds, 1 tsp black mustard seeds, 2 cardamom pods, 6 whole cloves, and 2 tsp ground turmeric and cook for 1 minute. Add 1¼ cups basmati rice and stir until coated. Pour in 2½ cups boiling water and some salt, then bring to the boil. Cover, then very gently simmer for 12–15 minutes, until all of the water has been absorbed.

Couscous is made from wheat flour that is mixed with water and rolled into grains.

Marvelous Moorish veggies

It's easy to adapt this recipe to make a vegetarian tagine. In the oil, with the onion and garlic, fry 1 small diced sweet potato, 1 quartered head of fennel, 8 halved new potatoes, 1 coarsely chopped red bell pepper, and chunks of 1 small eggplant and 2 zucchini. Cook for 5 minutes. Stir in the spices, vegetable stock, and tomatoes and cook for 1 hour. Stir in the rest of the ingredients with a 14 oz (400 g) can chickpeas and cook for a further 20 minutes.

Lamb tagine

This North African recipe is named after the special dome-shaped dish that it is traditionally cooked in, but it works just as well in a Dutch oven. It's usually served with couscous, but if you don't have any, use rice instead.

Top Tip
The meat should be so tender that it falls apart. If it is still a little tough after step 2, simmer for an extra 20 minutes before adding the dried fruit.

SERVES 4
PREPARATION: 20 MINUTES
COOKING: 2 HOURS
  20 MINUTES

2 tbsp sunflower oil
1 lb (450 g) lean lamb, cut into
  2-in (5-cm) pieces
1 onion, finely chopped
1 garlic clove, finely chopped
1-in (2.5-cm) piece fresh
  ginger, peeled and grated
1 tsp ground cinnamon
1 tsp ground cumin
1 tsp ground coriander seed
salt and freshly ground
  black pepper
1¼ cups lamb or
  vegetable stock
4 tomatoes, quartered
4 oz (115 g) dried apricots or
  pitted prunes, halved
2 oz (60 g) whole
  blanched almonds
½ lemon, juice only
1 tbsp honey

For the couscous
1½ cups couscous
2 tbsp olive oil

1 Heat the oil in a heavy flameproof Dutch oven and lightly brown the lamb on all sides. Stir in the onion, garlic, ginger, and spices and cook for another 2 minutes.

2 Season with salt and pepper, then add the stock and tomatoes. Bring to the boil, then reduce the heat to low. Cover the pan and simmer for 1¾–2 hours, stirring every 30 minutes, or until the meat is very tender.

3 Add the apricots or prunes, almonds, lemon juice, and honey. Bring to the boil, then reduce the heat and simmer for a further 20 minutes, adding extra stock if the sauce becomes too thick.

4 Place the couscous in a large bowl and pour over 1¼ cups boiling water. Stir, cover with plastic wrap, and leave to rest for 5 minutes.

5 Fluff up the couscous grains with a fork, then drizzle over the olive oil and gently mix through. Serve with the tagine.

Chili con carne

This is a great dish to feed a crowd, and you cook it in one big pot. Make the chili the day before you need it—the flavors will improve overnight—so all that's left to do is reheat it and cook the rice.

SERVES 4
PREPARATION: 25 MINUTES
COOKING: 45 MINUTES

3 tbsp olive oil

2 onions, chopped

3 garlic cloves, finely chopped

2 green chilies, finely chopped, or 2 tsp dried chili flakes

1 red bell pepper, deseeded and diced

1 tsp ground cumin

2 tsp paprika

1 tsp dried oregano

2¼ cups ground beef

2 tbsp tomato paste

14 oz (400 g) can red kidney beans, drained and rinsed

2 bay leaves

14 oz (400 g) can chopped tomatoes

2¼ cups beef stock

salt and freshly ground black pepper

small bunch fresh cilantro, chopped

To serve
sour cream
1 lime, cut into wedges

1 Heat the olive oil in a large heavy pan and gently fry the onions, garlic, and chilies for 5 minutes until softened. Add the red bell pepper, spices, and oregano and cook for another 2 minutes.

2 Turn the heat up to high, add the ground beef, and cook, breaking it up with a wooden spoon for 3–4 minutes until browned. Add the tomato paste and cook for another 2 minutes.

3 Add the kidney beans, bay leaves, tomatoes, and just enough stock to cover. Stir well, season with salt and pepper, and bring to the boil. Reduce the heat, cover, and simmer for 45 minutes, stirring occasionally.

4 Stir through the chopped cilantro and spoon the chili over cooked rice. Serve with the lime wedges, to squeeze over the chili, and sour cream to tone down the heat.

Look out for jalapeño chilies—they have a fragrant flavor and are not too hot!

Top Tip
If there's any chili left over, use it to make burritos. Just heat up the meat and spoon it onto flour tortillas with guacamole, sour cream, and some grated cheese. Roll them up and enjoy!

For a little crunch, scoop up the chili with tortilla chips.

Chili without carne
Chili con carne is Spanish for "chili with meat," but don't let this stop you from making a vegetarian version. Replace the meat with 1 deseeded, finely chopped green bell pepper and add an extra 14 oz (400 g) can of different beans in step 3. There are lots of different types—black-eyed peas, pinto beans, cannellini beans, or even chickpeas. Use vegetable stock instead of beef.

Guacamole (see page 30) is great with chili con carne.

49

Top Tip
To make bread crumbs, tear stale bread into pieces and pulse them in a food processor or rub thick slices against the large holes of a cheese grater.

Garnish the dish with a sprig of fresh parsley.

Tapas feast
Tapas is the name for a light meal made up of many small dishes that you share. Make your own tapas party by serving the meatballs with other dishes such as Spanish omelet (see pages 20–21), empanadas (pages 98–99), fried chorizo, sliced Manchego cheese, and lots of bread.

Spanish meatballs

Meatballs are popular all over the world, and each country has its own special recipe. They can be fried, steamed, served in a soup, or even stuffed with cheese. These spicy meatballs in tomato sauce are found in Spain and Latin America.

SERVES 6
PREPARATION: 30 MINUTES
COOKING: 25 MINUTES

2 onions, finely chopped
1 cup packed ground pork
1 cup packed ground beef
1 tsp dried oregano
1 cup fresh white
  bread crumbs
1 tsp ground cumin
½ tsp grated nutmeg
1 egg, beaten
salt and freshly ground
  black pepper
5 tbsp olive oil
2 garlic cloves, finely chopped
pinch of chili powder
2 x 14 oz (400 g) cans
  chopped tomatoes
½ cup vegetable stock

1 Place half of the onions, the pork and beef, oregano, bread crumbs, cumin, nutmeg, and egg into a large bowl. Mix well and then season with salt and freshly ground black pepper.

2 Using slightly damp hands, roll the meat mixture into balls about 2 in (5 cm) across.

3 Heat 3 tbsp of the olive oil in a frying pan and gently fry the meatballs for 5–6 minutes, turning regularly, until completely browned. Remove from the pan and set aside.

4 To make the sauce, heat the rest of the olive oil in the pan over medium heat and gently fry the remaining onions, the garlic, and chili powder until soft and golden.

5 Add the chopped tomatoes, season with salt and pepper, and cook for 5–6 minutes.

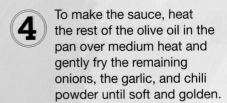

6 Add the stock to the sauce and stir well, then drop in the meatballs. Simmer for 25 minutes, or until the sauce is thick and the meatballs are cooked through. Serve with rice or crusty bread to soak up the rich tomato sauce.

Chicken paprikash

This stew is a Hungarian recipe and a great winter warmer. The simple ingredients are transformed by the spice paprika, made from dried sweet peppers, which gives the dish its wonderful flavor and color.

SERVES 4
PREPARATION: 20 MINUTES
COOKING: 45–55 MINUTES

8 boneless chicken thighs
salt and freshly ground
   black pepper
2 tbsp olive oil
2 red onions, chopped
2 garlic cloves, finely chopped
2 tbsp paprika
¼ tsp caraway seeds
1 cup chicken stock
1 tbsp red wine vinegar
1 tbsp tomato paste
1 tsp sugar
2 red bell peppers, sliced
9 oz (250 g) cherry tomatoes
1 small handful fresh parsley,
   finely chopped
⅔ cup sour cream

1 Season the chicken with salt and freshly ground black pepper. Heat 1 tbsp of the oil in a large flameproof Dutch oven over medium heat and brown the chicken for 5 minutes. Transfer to a large plate and set aside.

2 Heat the rest of the oil in the pan and fry the onions and garlic for about 5 minutes, or until the onions have softened. Stir in the paprika and caraway seeds, then return the chicken to the pot.

3 Mix together the stock, vinegar, tomato paste, and sugar. Pour over the chicken and bring to the boil. Season, then reduce to low heat, cover, and simmer for 30–40 minutes, or until the chicken is tender.

4 Add the bell peppers and cherry tomatoes and stir to mix everything together. Cover and simmer for a further 15 minutes.

5 Remove from the heat and top with the parsley and spoonfuls of sour cream. Serve with some cooked rice, potatoes, or buttered noodles.

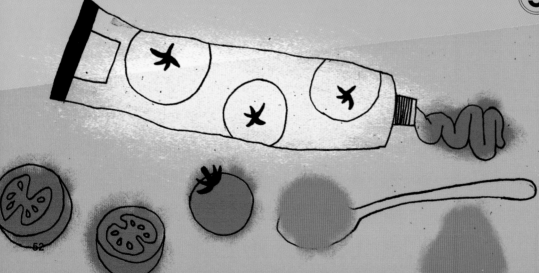

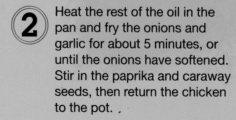

Pork paprikash

This recipe is also good with pork. Cut 1 lb (450 g) pork tenderloin into 1-in (2.5-cm) cubes and brown as you would the chicken thighs. Proceed as in the original recipe, but in step 3, simmer the stew for only 20 minutes. Add the bell peppers and tomatoes as in step 4, then cook for a further 10 minutes before adding the parsley and sour cream.

Top Tip
If you don't have fresh tomatoes, you can use a 14 oz (400 g) can of chopped tomatoes instead.

Fish cakes

Crispy on the outside but soft on the inside, these salmon fish cakes are a real treat. Prepare them ahead of time, keep them in the fridge, then cook them up when you're ready to eat. Serve with a simple green salad.

MAKES 8 FISH CAKES
PREPARATION: 45 MINUTES,
  PLUS CHILLING
COOKING: 6–8 MINUTES

1 lb 5 oz (600 g) potatoes, peeled
  and cut into large chunks
salt and freshly ground
  black pepper
1 lb (450 g) salmon fillets
milk, to cover fish
1 bay leaf
1 lemon—1 strip of zest
  (use a potato peeler for this)
  and wedges for garnish
3 tbsp fresh chopped parsley
4 scallions, chopped
7 oz (200 g) day-old white bread,
  crusts removed
4 tbsp all-purpose flour,
  plus extra for dusting
1 large egg, beaten
2 tbsp olive oil

Instead of fresh salmon, you can use the same quantity of smoked salmon, or canned salmon or tuna.

1 Cook the potatoes in boiling salted water for 20 minutes, or until tender when pierced with a knife. Drain in a colander, then put back into the pan.

2 Meanwhile, place the salmon in a small pan with enough milk to cover. Add the bay leaf and strip of lemon zest, place the pan over medium heat, and let the milk come slowly to the boil. Cook for 1 minute, then cover with a lid and turn off the heat. Set aside to cool. The fish should now be opaque pink.

3 Mash the potatoes with a masher or fork, adding 2 tbsp of the milk in which the fish was poached. Lift the fish out of the milk, remove any skin and bones, and flake into a large bowl.

4 Add the mashed potatoes, parsley, scallions, and plenty of salt and freshly ground pepper. Finely grate over the remaining lemon zest and mix everything together well.

5 Divide the mixture into 8 and shape each one into a ¾-in (2-cm) thick cake using a little flour to stop it from sticking to your hands. Place on a plate and put them in the fridge to get firm for 30 minutes.

6 Put the bread into a blender or food processor and pulse until it forms crumbs, then tip on to a plate. Put the egg on to another plate and the flour onto another.

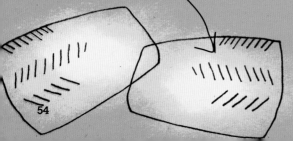

7 Coat all of the cakes in the flour, then the egg, and then the crumbs. Keep in the refrigerator until ready to cook.

8 Heat the olive oil in a large frying pan. Add the fish cakes and cook for 3–4 minutes on each side until golden. If you can't fit them all in the pan together, keep the first batch hot in the oven while cooking the rest. Serve with the lemon wedges to squeeze over and a green salad.

Top Tip
If you don't want to fry the fish cakes, put them in the oven at 425 °F (220 °C) for 15 minutes, then to crisp them up, put them under a hot broiler until golden, turning once.

Pad Thai

Served from food carts all around Thailand, Pad Thai is the ultimate street food. Some of the ingredients sound unusual, but you should be able to find them in large supermarkets.

Top Tip
A wok is the perfect pan for stir-frying, but if you don't have one, use a big frying pan instead.

SERVES 4
PREPARATION: 15 MINUTES
COOKING: 5–6 MINUTES

12 oz (350 g) flat rice noodles
2 tbsp fresh chopped cilantro
1 red chili, deseeded and
  finely chopped
1 garlic clove, finely chopped
4 tbsp sunflower oil
9 oz (250 g) raw
  peeled shrimp
5 shallots, finely chopped
2 eggs, beaten
1 tbsp light brown sugar
1 tbsp oyster sauce
1 tbsp Thai fish sauce
juice of 1 lime
2 tbsp sweet chili sauce
4½ cups fresh bean sprouts
4 scallions, sliced
1 lime, cut into wedges, to serve

1 Prepare the noodles according to the instructions on the package and set aside. Mix together the cilantro, chili, and garlic with the oil in a bowl.

2 Heat half of the oil mixture in a wok. When very hot, add the shrimp and stir-fry for 1 minute until pink, then remove from the pan and set aside.

3 Add the remaining oil mixture and fry the shallots for 1 minute. Add the eggs and sugar and cook for 1 minute, stirring to scramble the eggs.

4 Stir in the oyster sauce, fish sauce, lime juice, sweet chili sauce, cooked rice noodles, and bean sprouts and stir-fry for 2 minutes.

5 Return the shrimp to the wok with the scallions and mix together for 1–2 minutes, or until everything is piping hot. Serve with the lime wedges on the side.

Chinese pork stir-fry

For the perfect stir-fry, cut the ingredients into equal-size pieces, so that they take the same time to cook, get the wok hot, and keep the food moving by constantly stirring.

SERVES 4
PREPARATION: 15 MINUTES,
  PLUS 15 MINUTES
  MARINATING
COOKING: 6–7 MINUTES

14 oz (400 g) pork fillet,
  finely sliced
1 tbsp Chinese rice vinegar
1 tbsp soy sauce
2 tsp sesame oil
1 tsp cornstarch
7 oz (200 g) bok choy
1-in (2.5-cm) piece fresh
  ginger, peeled and grated
1 garlic clove, finely sliced
2 tbsp sunflower oil
3 tbsp oyster sauce

3 Heat the sunflower oil in a wok until very hot and slightly smoking. Add the pork mixture and stir-fry for 2–3 minutes, or until brown, then remove to a plate.

1 Place the pork in a bowl with the rice vinegar, soy sauce, sesame oil, and cornstarch. Stir to completely coat the meat, then set aside to marinate for 15 minutes.

2 Meanwhile, cut the leaves off the bok choy and set aside. Chop the stalks into ¾-in (2-cm) slices.

4 Add the ginger and garlic to the wok and stir-fry for 1–2 minutes, or until golden. Add the bok choy stalks and stir-fry for 2 minutes, then add the leaves, oyster sauce, and 3–4 tbsp water and continue cooking until the sauce starts bubbling.

5 Return the pork to the wok and heat through for 1–2 minutes. Serve with steamed rice.

If you can't find bok choy, use cabbage or broccoli.

Cannelloni

This is a vegetarian dish made of large tubes of pasta filled with spinach and ricotta—a light curd cheese from Italy. Traditionally, cannelloni is topped with a white sauce. This recipe uses crème fraîche instead, as a shortcut.

Top Tip
If you can't find crème fraîche in the supermarket, you can use the same quantity of sour cream for the topping instead.

SERVES 4
PREPARATION: 35 MINUTES
COOKING: 45–55 MINUTES

pat of butter
olive oil
2 garlic cloves, finely sliced
1 lb 2 oz (500 g) fresh spinach
   leaves, washed
1⅓ cups ricotta cheese
1 egg, beaten
½ cup freshly grated
   Parmesan cheese
¼ tsp grated nutmeg
salt and freshly ground
   black pepper
16 cannelloni tubes
2 x 14 oz (400 g) cans
   chopped tomatoes
pinch of sugar
handful of fresh basil
   leaves, torn
2¼ cups crème fraîche
2 tbsp water
7 oz (200 g) mozzarella cheese,
   torn into pieces

1 Preheat the oven to 350°F (180°C). Heat the butter and a drizzle of olive oil in a large saucepan and fry one of the sliced garlic cloves until soft. Stir in the spinach, a handful at a time, until it has all wilted. Remove the pan from the heat.

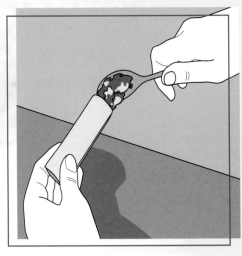

2 When cool, drain the spinach in a strainer, squeezing well to remove any excess water. Chop finely then place in a bowl and mix in the ricotta, beaten egg, and half of the Parmesan cheese. Season with the grated nutmeg, salt, and freshly ground black pepper.

3 Use a teaspoon to scoop the ricotta mixture into the cannelloni tubes so that each one is completely filled up. Lay the tubes close together in a lightly oiled baking dish.

4 Place the saucepan back on the heat and soften the rest of the garlic in a little olive oil. Pour in the tomatoes and bring to the boil. Add the sugar and season with salt and freshly ground black pepper, then reduce the heat and simmer for 15 minutes, or until the sauce has thickened. Stir in the basil leaves, then pour the sauce over the cannelloni.

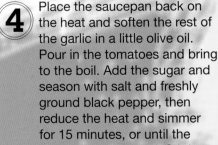

When ready, the top of the cannelloni should be golden and bubbly.

5 In a bowl, mix together the crème fraîche, the rest of the Parmesan cheese, some salt and freshly ground black pepper, and the water. Spoon the sauce over the tomato layer, top with the mozzarella cheese, then bake in the oven for 30–40 minutes, until the cannelloni is tender when pierced with a knife.

Cannelloni for carnivores

For meaty cannelloni, fill the pasta tubes with the Bolognese sauce from page 61. Top with the tomato sauce, crème fraîche, mozzarella, and a handful of Parmesan, and bake as above.

Pasta sauces

There is an amazing array of pasta shapes and sauces to try. Don't buy sauce in jar—make your own! The flavors will taste so much fresher. These classic recipes are quick and easy, so you can use them again and again. All recipes serve 4.

spaghetti

penne

farfalle

Pasta shapes usually go with chunky sauces, and spaghetti and tagliatelle are best with thin sauces.

Tomato sauce
Fry 2 finely chopped garlic cloves and 1 chopped onion in a little olive oil. Stir in a 14 oz (400 g) can of chopped tomatoes, 1 tbsp tomato paste, and a pinch of sugar. Bring to the boil, then reduce the heat and simmer for 25 minutes, or until the sauce has thickened. Add a handful of torn fresh basil and season with salt and freshly ground black pepper. Cook 10 oz (300 g) dried pasta shapes and serve topped with the sauce.

Spaghetti carbonara
Fry 6 chopped slices of bacon and 1 finely chopped garlic clove in a little olive oil. Beat together 4 egg yolks, ⅔ cup light cream, ½ cup grated Parmesan cheese, and plenty of freshly ground black pepper. Cook 14 oz (400 g) dried spaghetti. Drain, then return to the pan and toss with the bacon and egg mixture until the pasta is evenly coated.

Use half and half and replace the bacon with lean ham for a healthier carbonara.

Pesto

Toast 3 tbsp pine kernels in a dry frying pan, stirring until golden. Set aside. Put 4½ oz (125 g) fresh basil, 2 finely chopped garlic cloves, 6 tbsp olive oil, and the cooled pine kernels in a food processor and pulse until blended to a coarse purée. Add 7 tbsp finely grated Parmesan cheese and pulse again. Cook 14 oz (400 g) dried pasta. Drain, then return to the pan and stir in the pesto.

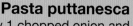

To bulk up pasta with pesto, add cooked vegetables, such as broccoli or mushrooms.

Pasta puttanesca

Fry 1 chopped onion and 1 finely chopped garlic clove in a little olive oil until soft. Add 1 deseeded and chopped red chili, 1¾ oz (50 g) drained canned anchovies, 6 oz (175 g) chopped black olives, 1 tbsp capers, and a 14 oz (400 g) can chopped tomatoes. Bring to the boil and simmer for 20 minutes, or until thickened. Cook 14 oz (400 g) dried pasta and toss through the sauce.

Bolognese sauce

Fry 2 finely chopped garlic cloves, 1 chopped onion, 2 chopped celery ribs, and 1 grated carrot in a little olive oil for 5 minutes. Pour in 2½ cups ground beef and cook, stirring, until browned. Add a 14 oz (400 g) can chopped tomatoes, 2 tbsp tomato paste, 1¼ cups water, a beef bouillon cube, and 1 tsp dried oregano. Season with salt and freshly ground black pepper, then simmer for 45 minutes. Cook 14 oz (400 g) dried spaghetti and serve topped with the sauce.

Lamb kebabs

Top Tip
For really flavorful and tender kebabs, prepare them the day before and leave the meat to marinate overnight.

These tasty kebabs are fantastic on the grill, but if it rains, just cook them under the broiler inside. You can use cubes of chicken or fish instead of lamb if you prefer.

SERVES 4
PREPARATION: 20 MINUTES,
** PLUS MARINATING**
COOKING: 12–14 MINUTES

For the kebabs

1 lb 2 oz (500 g) lamb
  shoulder, cut into 1½-in
  (4-cm) cubes
1 red bell pepper, deseeded
  and cut into bite-size chunks
1 red onion, cut into
  bite-size chunks

For the marinade

2 garlic cloves, finely chopped
1 tsp chili flakes or powder
1 tsp ground cumin
1 tsp ground cinnamon
1 tsp ground coriander seed
1 tbsp honey
handful of fresh mint leaves,
  finely chopped
1 tbsp olive oil
juice of ½ lemon

1 Mix all of the marinade ingredients together in a nonmetallic bowl. Add the lamb and toss gently to completely coat the meat. Cover and refrigerate for at least 2 hours.

2 Meanwhile, soak 4 wooden skewers in water to prevent them from catching on fire during broiling or grilling. Or you can use metal ones if you have them.

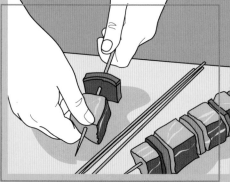

3 Thread the cubes of lamb onto the skewers, alternating with pieces of bell pepper and onion. Preheat the broiler or get the grill hot.

4 Broil or grill the kebabs for 12–14 minutes, turning every few minutes. The meat should be brown on the outside but still pink and juicy inside. Slide the meat and vegetables off the skewers with a fork, then stuff them in pitas or serve with a salad or rice.

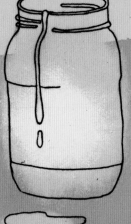

Scatter with fresh mint and sliced chilies before serving for extra color, flavor, and spice.

Minus the meat
For a vegetarian alternative, replace the meat with pieces of cubed eggplant and zucchini, halloumi cheese, or all three.

Barbecue food

Here are some great recipes for the grill. When cooking on coals, getting the timing right can be tricky, so if you're entertaining, make sure you've got lots of other food that doesn't need to be cooked, such as salads (see pages 18–19), dips (pages 30–31), and garlic bread (page 36).

BBQ ribs (serves 4)

Simmer 2¼ lb (1 kg) pork spareribs in salted water for 30 minutes, then drain, rinse, and leave to cool. In a saucepan, bring to the boil 8 tbsp ketchup, 1 tbsp brown sugar, 2 tbsp Worcestershire sauce, 1 tbsp apple cider vinegar, 2 tsp prepared mustard, ½ tsp smoked paprika, and 1 finely chopped garlic clove and simmer for 5 minutes. When cooled, brush all over the ribs and grill for 8–10 minutes, turning and coating with sauce regularly.

You can pour BBQ sauce onto burgers, too.

Best burgers (makes 4)

Fry ½ a finely chopped red onion and 2 finely chopped garlic cloves in 1 tbsp olive oil until soft, then leave to cool. Mix the onion into 2½ cups ground beef with 1 tsp chili powder, a large pinch of salt, and freshly ground black pepper. Shape into 4 burgers and grill for about 6–8 minutes, turning once. Top each with a slice of cheese and, when it starts to melt, serve in a warm roll.

For extra flavor, add fresh chopped herbs such as parsley, thyme, or basil to the burger mix.

Put thin strips of vegetables, such as carrots and zucchini, inside your fish packages for a meal in one.

Fish foil packages

To barbecue salmon fillets, put each one in a foil package with sprigs of thyme or tarragon, orange zest, slices of lemon, and salt and pepper. Seal and grill for 4–5 minutes. You can also cook whole fish in foil, such as sardines, mackerel, or sea bass up to 9 oz (250 g). Add a squeeze of lime juice and ¼ tsp each of grated fresh ginger, chopped garlic, and chopped red chili. Grill for 6–8 minutes. Test that the fish is cooked with a knife—it should flake away easily.

Shrimp skewers with peanut dip (serves 4)

Mix 1 tbsp olive oil with 2 finely chopped garlic cloves, the juice of ½ a lime, and 1 tbsp soy sauce. Add 1 lb (450 g) raw peeled shrimp and marinate in the fridge for 15 minutes. Meanwhile, make the dip. Whisk 5 tbsp smooth peanut butter with 3 fl oz (90 ml) boiling water, 1 finely chopped garlic clove, 2 tbsp lime juice, 2 tbsp soy sauce, 1 tbsp sweet chili sauce, and a pinch of salt and pepper. Thread the shrimp onto skewers and grill for 2–3 minutes on each side.

Grilled eggplants (serves 2)

Combine 2 tbsp clear honey, 3 tbsp olive oil, 2 tsp apple cider vinegar, 2 tsp Dijon mustard, and 2 bruised and halved garlic cloves with 1 tbsp fresh oregano.
Cut 2 small eggplants in half lengthwise and rub the marinade over well. Season with salt and freshly ground black pepper, then grill for 8–10 minutes until tender.
Serve with fresh tomato salsa (see page 31).

Caramelized fruit (serves 4)

Mix 3 tbsp clear honey with 1 tbsp lemon juice, 2 tbsp melted butter, and 1 tsp ground cinnamon. Thread thick slices of fresh fruit onto soaked wooden skewers—pineapple, apples, peaches, and pears are all delicious—and brush with the glaze. On a clean area of the grill, cook for 2–3 minutes on each side until golden.

The hot fruit is delicious with cold ice cream.

Something sweet

The finishing touch to a great meal is something sweet—for many, it's the best part! It's fun to make a spectacular dessert for a special occasion—perhaps something chocolaty or a creamy cheesecake. But for every day meals, there are lots of quick tricks for turning simple ingredients, such as fruit or ice cream, into delicious desserts.

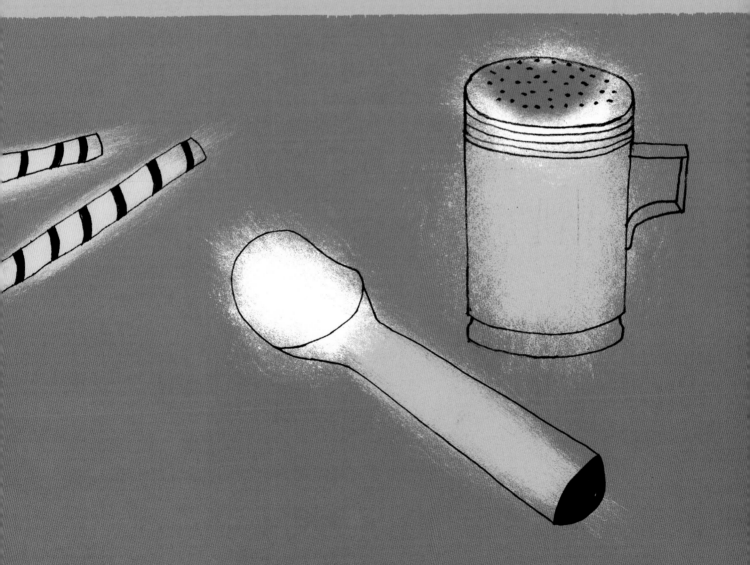

Fruit meringue

If you want a spectacular dessert, meringue never fails to impress. This mixture of fruit, whipped cream, and crunchy baked egg whites is irresistible and is great for a party as you can make it ahead of time and assemble it at the last minute.

Top Tip
To make meringue, you need a mixer with a whisk attachment, or an electric hand whisk. You can use a balloon whisk, but it's very hard work!

SERVES 8
PREPARATION: 30 MINUTES
COOKING: 1¼–1¾ HOURS

4 egg whites
1 cup superfine sugar
2½ cups heavy cream
2 kiwifruit, peeled and sliced
1 lb (450 g) fresh strawberries
4 passion fruit

For a lower-fat filling, replace I cup of the heavy cream with low-fat plain yogurt.

1 Heat the oven to 300°F (150°C). Line a large cookie sheet with parchment paper and, using a dinner plate as a guide, draw a large circle on it.

2 Put the egg whites in a very clean large mixing bowl—they're going to increase dramatically in volume. Whisk until they form soft peaks.

3 Add a tablespoonful of sugar and whisk for 1 minute. Continue adding sugar and then whisking until all of the sugar is used and the mixture is smooth. The meringue should stand in stiff peaks when you lift out the whisk.

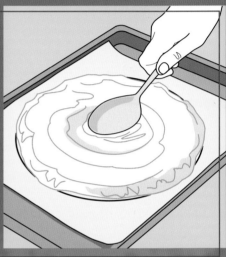

4 Spoon the mixture into the circle on the parchment paper and push it out to the edge. Slightly hollow out the center. Bake for 15 minutes, then lower the temperature to 275°F (140°C) and continue to cook for a further 1–1½ hours, or until crisp. Leave to cool.

5 Assemble the dessert no more than 2 hours before you're going to eat it. Whip the cream to form soft peaks, then spread it over the meringue. Arrange the fruit on top, scoop the passion-fruit seeds, scatter them over the fruit, and serve.

Put any fresh fruit that you like on top—raspberries, blueberries, or peaches.

You can make the meringue base ahead of time and keep it in an airtight container for up to a week.

If you'd rather make lots of small meringues, just scoop dessert-spoonfuls of the mixture onto a lined cookie sheet and bake for 1-1½ hours. When cool, sandwich two together with whipped cream.

It's a mess!

A great way to use store-bought meringues, or broken homemade ones, is to make what's officially called a "mess." Break into chunks and mix with lightly whipped cream and fruit that has been cut into small pieces or mashed. Spoon into glasses and eat right away.

Fruit feast

Fruit is delicious, nutritious, and versatile, so you don't have to do much to turn it into something special. Always use fruit that is ripe, it will be sweeter and have much more flavor. Feel free to adapt the recipes below to use your favorite fruits or what is in season.

Chocolate fruit
Melt 2½ cups chocolate chips and 3 tbsp heavy cream in a bowl set over a pan of simmering water. Stir until smooth, then spoon the chocolate sauce into small bowls. Serve with strawberries, or any fruit that you'd like to dip in.

Strawberry popsicles (makes 6)
Wash and hull 7 oz (200 g) strawberries, then put them in a food processor with 2 tbsp confectioners' sugar. Pulse, then strain the purée into a bowl and discard the seeds. Mix the purée with 1¾ cups plain yogurt and add extra confectioners' sugar to taste. Pour the mixture into 6 popsicle molds and freeze for about 3 hours, or until frozen.

Fruit kebabs (makes 6)
It's fun to present fruit on skewers. Peel and slice into chunks 2 kiwifruit and 2 small bananas, and slice 12 large strawberries in half. Thread the fruit on to 6 wooden skewers, then brush them with orange juice mixed with a little honey. This will prevent fruit like banana and apples from going brown. You can use any fruits, so mix and match your favorites—pineapple, peaches, and melons all work well.

Fruit salad (serves 6)

Fruit salads work with all kinds of fruit combinations, but this one is a sure-fire winner. Remove the hulls and halve 9 oz (250 g) strawberries and place in a large bowl. Cut ½ a honeydew melon and ½ a cantaloupe into bite-size chunks and add them to the bowl with a peeled and segmented tangerines, 4½ oz (125 g) raspberries, and 9 oz (250 g) seedless black grapes. Sprinkle over a little superfine sugar, then chill until you are ready to eat.

Banana is fantastic baked with chocolate. Make a cut in the fruit lengthwise, press into chunks of chocolate, wrap in foil, and bake for 20 minutes in a preheated oven set at 350°F (180°C).

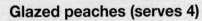

Glazed peaches (serves 4)

Cut 4 ripe peaches in half and remove their pits. Mix together 2 tbsp light brown sugar with ¼ tsp ground cinnamon, scatter over the peaches, and place under the broiler. Cook for about 5 minutes, or until they are golden and bubbling on top. Serve with a dollop of Greek yogurt with some maple syrup, and pecan nuts scattered over.

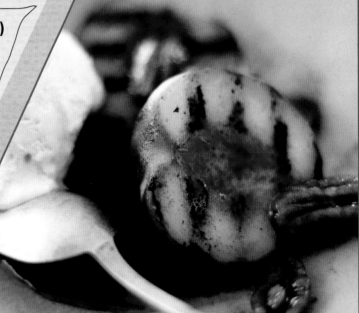

Strawberry fool

This combination of fresh fruit and whipped cream is an easy way to prepare a delicious dessert. This no-cook recipe has few ingredients, so you can make it when you are in a hurry.

Top Tip
For a lower-fat version, stir ⅔ cup light cream with 2¼ cups of nonfat Greek yogurt, instead of the heavy cream. Stir in the mashed strawberries and top with amaretti crumbs.

SERVES 4
PREPARATION: 15 MINUTES,
 PLUS CHILLING

9 oz (250 g) strawberries, hulled
2 tbsp confectioners' sugar
1 tbsp lemon juice
1¼ cups heavy cream
2 amaretti cookies, crushed

1) Use a fork or potato masher to mash the strawberries, confectioners' sugar, and lemon juice until soft and pulpy.

2) Whip the cream until soft peaks form, then fold the mashed fruit into the cream until it is marbled throughout.

3) Divide the mixture into 4 glasses and chill in the refrigerator for 1–2 hours.

4) Once chilled, sprinkle the amaretti cookie crumbs over the top and serve.

For a smoother fool, pulse the fruit in a blender before adding to the cream.

For a pretty finishing touch, decorate with a sprig of fresh mint.

Chocolate mousse

This classic French recipe is delicious but very rich, so serve it up in small portions. Note that the dessert contains raw eggs, and should not be eaten by very young children or the elderly (see page 8).

SERVES 6
PREPARATION: 20 MINUTES,
** PLUS CHILLING**

7 oz (200 g) dark chocolate,
  broken into pieces
3 tbsp butter
3 eggs, separated
3 tbsp superfine sugar

Top Tip
It is a good idea to chill the chocolate mousse for about 2 hours before serving. This allows the chocolate to set and gives it a rich and velvety texture.

1 Place the chocolate in a heatproof bowl over a pan of simmering water. When the chocolate has melted, add the butter and stir until smooth. Remove from the heat and allow to cool slightly.

2 Beat the egg yolks into the mixture one at a time.

3 Whisk the eggs whites until they form stiff peaks, then whisk in the superfine sugar. Stir some of the egg whites into the chocolate mixture and gently fold in the rest.

4 Spoon into small bowls or cups and chill for at least 2 hours.

If you like, top with fresh raspberries.

Use mint-flavored chocolate to give the mousse a new twist.

Stir 2 crumbled choc-chip cookies through the ice cream at the end of step 5, and you'll have choc-chip cookie ice cream!

Very berry nice

To add a ripple of fruit, mash 8 oz (225 g) strawberries or raspberries with 2 tbsp confectioners' sugar. Press through a strainer to remove the seeds, then stir the purée gently through the vanilla ice cream after you have whisked it for the last time at end of step 5.

Vanilla ice cream

Sweet, creamy, and deliciously cold, ice cream is always a treat, but homemade ice cream is even better, so learn how to make your own—it's not difficult and you don't need an ice cream maker. This recipe uses an electric hand whisk instead.

SERVES 6
PREPARATION: 20 MINUTES,
PLUS FREEZING

½ vanilla bean, split
⅓ cup whole milk
2 egg yolks
4 tbsp superfine sugar
1¼ cups heavy cream

To split a vanilla bean, cut down it lengthwise with a small sharp knife.

1 Split the vanilla bean, scrape out the seeds, then put the bean and seeds into a pan with the milk and heat to simmering point. Remove from the heat and take out the bean. In a separate bowl, whisk the egg yolks and sugar together until pale, then pour in the milk and whisk again.

2 Return the mixture to a clean, pan and cook over low heat, stirring constantly, until it thickens to the consistency of heavy cream and coats the back of the wooden spoon. Don't be impatient and turn up the heat or the mixture will curdle.

3 Cover the surface of the custard with plastic wrap, to stop a skin from forming, and set aside to cool.

4 Pour the heavy cream into a bowl and whisk until it forms soft peaks. Fold into the cold custard and pour into a freezer container.

5 Freeze for 2 hours, or until half frozen. Whisk with an electric hand whisk to break up the ice crystals. Half-freeze and whisk twice more, then leave to freeze completely.

Top Tip
Homemade ice cream freezes much harder than store bought, so leave it to soften in the fridge for 30 minutes before serving.

Ice cream fun

If you've got some ice cream in the freezer, it's easy to invent a cool dessert. As the recipes below show, it doesn't have to be complicated, all you need is some fruit, or some chocolate, and a bit of imagination. For the ultimate finishing touch, make a sweet sauce.

For a bit of fun, squirt some whipped cream on top.

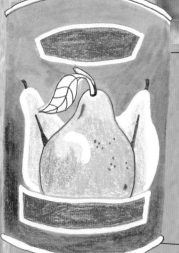

Chocolate pears (makes 1)

Spoon vanilla ice cream on to a small plate and top with two halves of canned or poached pears in syrup. Spoon over some of the syrup from the can and then drizzle over some chocolate sauce (see recipe opposite).

Fruit sundaes (makes 2)

Place 1 scoop of vanilla ice cream into 2 tall glasses. Mash 8 strawberries with 2 tsp confectioners' sugar and spoon into the glasses. Spoon 2 tbsp strawberry yogurt into each, then add a mix of fresh fruit such as chopped kiwifruit, sliced mango, sliced banana, and fresh raspberries. Finish with another scoop of ice cream and some toasted slivered almonds.

Chocolate and hazelnut banana split (makes 1)

Split 1 banana in half and fill with 2 scoops of any ice cream of your choice—vanilla or chocolate-chip ice creams go well. Scatter over some toasted chopped filberts and drizzle with some chocolate or fudge sauce (see recipes opposite).

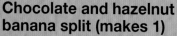

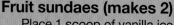

Chocolate sauce

Break 3½ oz (100 g) dark chocolate into small pieces and place in a saucepan with 4 tbsp hot water, and 3 tbsp superfine sugar. Stir over a low heat until the chocolate has melted, then add 4 tbsp heavy cream and heat through. Serve warm.

Make chocolate curls with a vegetable peeler.

Fudge sauce

Put ½ stick butter with ¼ cup light brown sugar in a pan with 2 tbsp light corn syrup. Bring to the boil, stirring gently, then boil rapidly for 1 minute. Stir in ½ cup heavy cream and a few drops of vanilla extract. Allow to cool slightly before serving.

For an instant dessert, put a scoop of ice cream on top of a cake, such as a muffin or waffle, and drizzle over some sauce.

Raspberry sauce

Put 12 oz (350 g) fresh raspberries in a food processor with 2 tbsp confectioners' sugar and 1 tbsp lemon juice. Blend until smooth, then pour into a strainer and press the liquid through with the back of a wooden spoon to remove all of the seeds. You can use this method with other soft berries such as strawberries and blackberries.

Little orange cakes

You can also make individual orange-chocolate cakes by grating the zest of 1 orange into the milk and chocolate as it is melting. Then use ramekins instead of one big dish and cook for 10 minutes less. Decorate with candied orange peel.

To get a very sticky cake, you need to cook it in a deep dish.

Chocolate dessert

This dessert is cooked in a pan of water, called a bain-marie, which gives a gentler heat. It is best eaten right away, while still light and fluffy on top and warm and gooey underneath.

SERVES 4
PREPARATION: 20 MINUTES,
** PLUS COOLING**
COOKING: 45–55 MINUTES

7 oz (200 g) dark chocolate,
  broken into pieces

7 fl oz (200 ml) whole milk

½ stick butter

5 tbsp superfine sugar

2 eggs, separated

½ cup self-rising flour, sifted

¼ cup cocoa powder, sifted

1 Preheat the oven to 350°F (180°C). Place the chocolate and milk in a saucepan and heat slowly, stirring until melted and smooth. Allow to cool slightly.

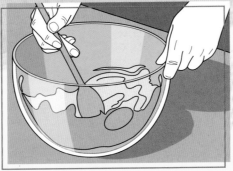

2 Beat together the butter and sugar, then beat in the egg yolks. Fold in the flour and cocoa powder. Add the warm chocolate mixture a little at a time.

3 In a separate bowl, whisk the egg whites until they are firm enough to stand up in stiff peaks.

4 Gently fold the egg whites into the chocolate mixture until they are combined, keeping as much air in the mixture as possible.

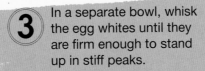

5 Spoon the mixture into a deep 5-cup ovenproof dish and place the dish in a baking pan. Half fill the pan with water so that it surrounds the dish.

6 Bake for 30–35 minutes, then cover loosely with foil and bake for a further 15–20 minutes. Serve while still warm and gooey.

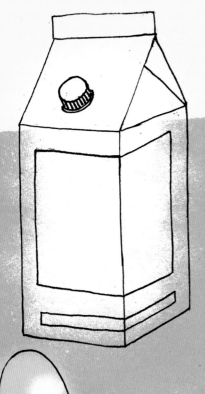

Tiramisu

The name of this Italian dessert means "pick me up," and the delicious mix of cream, chocolate, and coffee layers certainly will give you a lift! You need to chill tiramisu for a few hours before you eat it, to bring out the flavors.

Top Tip
You can also assemble the tiramisu ingredients in four glasses or bowls to make individual desserts.

SERVES 4

PREPARATION: 20 MINUTES, PLUS CHILLING

2 oz (60 g) dark chocolate

1 cup mascarpone

1 cup Greek yogurt

¼ cup superfine sugar

1 tsp vanilla extract

7 fl oz (200 ml) decaffeinated coffee, made with 1 tbsp instant decaffeinated coffee

20 ladyfingers

2 tsp cocoa powder

1 Grate the chocolate using a grater or food processor. Beat the mascarpone, Greek yogurt, superfine sugar, and vanilla extract together in a bowl until smooth and creamy.

2 Spoon one third of the mixture into the bottom of a serving bowl and spread it over evenly with the back of a wooden spoon.

3 Pour the coffee into a shallow bowl. Dip the ladyfingers into the coffee, and put a layer of them on top of the mixture in the serving bowl.

4 Sprinkle over 1 tbsp of the grated chocolate. Spoon half the remaining mascarpone mixture onto the chocolate-covered ladyfingers and smooth over gently. Top with another layer of dipped ladyfingers, and drizzle over any remaining coffee.

5 Sprinkle over 1 tbsp of the chocolate. Finish with the remaining mascarpone mixture, smoothing over the top evenly. Sift with cocoa powder and sprinkle with the remaining chocolate. Chill in the fridge for 2–3 hours.

The slightly bitter cocoa powder contrasts with the sweet creamy layers below.

Fruity tiramisu

For a lower-fat fruit tiramsu, beat 9 oz (250 g) low-fat plain yogurt with ⅔ cup nonfat Greek yogurt and 3 tbsp clear honey. Dip 10 ladyfingers in ⅔ cup orange juice and layer them in dessert glasses with the yogurt mixture and a layer of diced peaches or mangoes. Scatter toasted slivered almonds on top.

In England, crumble is traditionally served with vanilla custard.

The sugary fruit gets very hot, so leave the crumble to cool for 10 minutes before serving.

A feast of fruit

You can replace the fruit in this recipe with whatever is in season. In the summer months, try plums, nectarines, peaches, or apricots and mix with some soft fruit such as raspberries or strawberries. In late summer or early fall, use pears.

Fruit crumble

This easy-to-make dessert has long been a favorite. Served with whipped cream, ice cream, or yogurt, a simple fruit crumble tastes delicious, and fruit such as apples and blackberries are a good source of vitamins.

Top Tip
For a crunchy topping, replace 1¾ oz (50 g) of the flour with rolled oats. Just stir them into the crumble mixture with the sugar at the end of step 3.

SERVES 6
PREPARATION: 20 MINUTES
COOKING: 30 MINUTES

For the filling
4 cooking apples
8 oz (250 g) blackberries
¼ cup superfine sugar
½ tsp ground cinnamon

For the topping
1¾ cups all-purpose flour
1 stick unsalted butter, diced
1½ cup less tbsp superfine sugar
1 tbsp soft light brown sugar

1 Preheat the oven to 375°F (190°C). Peel the apples, then cut into quarters. Carefully remove the cores and cut into bite-size pieces.

2 Place the apples and blackberries in a baking dish and sprinkle over the sugar and cinnamon. Stir the fruit to ensure that they are coated evenly in the sugar mixture.

3 Put the flour into a mixing bowl and add the diced butter. Rub the butter into the flour, using your fingertips. When the butter is evenly mixed through the flour and the mixture starts to clump together, stir in the superfine sugar.

4 Scatter the crumble topping over the fruit and sprinkle the brown sugar on top.

5 Place the dish on a cookie sheet and bake for about 30 minutes, or until golden and the fruit juices bubble around the edges.

If fresh blackberries are not available, you can use canned, but drain the juice.

Profiteroles

These light chocolaty balls, filled with whipped cream look very professional, but don't let this scare you. The crispy shells are made of choux pastry, which is easy to make—and even easier to eat.

Top Tip
Choux pastry doesn't keep well, so don't make the profiteroles too far ahead. Only fill them a short time before you're going to eat them or they'll get soggy.

MAKES 12
PREPARATION: 30 MINUTES
COOKING: 25 MINUTES

⅔ cup all-purpose flour
1 tsp sugar
⅔ cup water
½ stick butter, plus extra
  for greasing
2 eggs, beaten

For the filling
1¼ cups heavy cream

For the sauce
5½ oz (150 g) dark chocolate
3½ tbsp butter

1 Preheat the oven to 400°F (200°C). Grease a cookie sheet. Sift the flour into a bowl with the sugar.

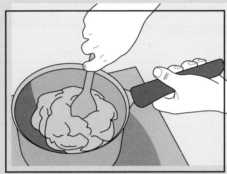

2 Put the water and butter in a pan over medium heat. When the butter has melted and the mixture begins to boil, remove from the heat. Quickly add the flour and sugar and beat with a wooden spoon until the pastry forms a smooth ball. Allow to cool for 1–2 minutes.

3 Add the beaten eggs a little at a time, thoroughly mixing them in before adding more, to make a thick, smooth, glossy paste.

4 Hold the greased cookie sheet under cold running water for a few seconds, then shake to leave it slightly damp. Then place walnut-size spoonfuls of the mixture on the sheet, leaving lots of space between them.

5 Bake in the oven for 25 minutes, or until the pastry is light, puffy, and golden. Put on a rack to cool and pierce the side of each pastry with a fork to let out the steam, to prevent them from getting soggy.

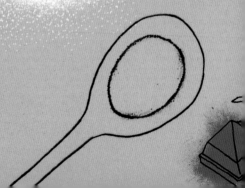

84

6 To make the chocolate sauce, break the chocolate into small pieces and put it in a pan with the butter. Melt over low heat, stirring until melted, and remove from the heat.

Try using ice cream instead of whipped cream to fill the pastry balls. Keep them in the freezer until ready to serve, then add the chocolate sauce.

7 Whip the cream until it forms soft peaks. Cut open the profiteroles and fill each one with cream. Arrange on a serving plate and pour over the chocolate sauce.

Chocolate éclairs

You can also turn choux pastry into éclairs. To make a pastry bag, spoon the mixture into a freezer bag and cut off a corner. Squeeze short lengths onto a cookie sheet, then bake at 400°F (200°C) for 20–25 minutes. Cut in half, lengthwise, cool, fill with whipped cream, and top with chocolate sauce.

Cherry cheesecake

A perfect summer treat, this no-cook cheesecake is very easy to prepare and is as tasty as it looks. Make it the day before you want to eat it, though—it needs to chill overnight.

SERVES 12
PREPARATION: 30 MINUTES,
  PLUS CHILLING OVERNIGHT

9 oz (250 g) graham crackers
1 stick butter
2⅔ cups cream cheese
½ cup packed
  confectioners' sugar
4 lemons, finely grated zest only
1 tsp vanilla extract
1¼ cups heavy cream
14 oz (400 g) can pitted
  black cherries

If you don't have graham crackers, use any plain sweet "oaty" or whole-meal cookie.

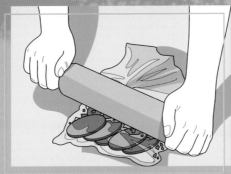

1 Grease and line the bottom of a 9-in (23-cm) loose-based pan with some butter and parchment paper. Put the crackers in a food bag, seal, and then crush them into crumbs using a rolling pin.

2 Melt the remaining butter in a pan over low heat, then add the crushed crackers, and mix until the crumbs are completely coated. Transfer the mixture to the pan, pressing down firmly to create an even layer. Chill in the fridge for about 1 hour to set firmly.

3 Mix the cream cheese, confectioners' sugar, lemon zest, and vanilla extract in a bowl, then beat with an electric mixer until smooth. Add the heavy cream and continue beating the mixture until smooth.

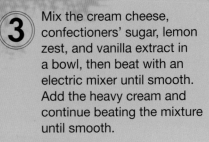

4 Pour the mixture onto the cracker base, spreading it out evenly with the back of a wooden spoon or spatula. Leave in the fridge overnight.

5 Drain the juice from the cherries into a saucepan. Bring the juice to the boil and simmer for 10 minutes, or until syrupy. Leave to cool.

6 Bring the cheesecake to room temperature about 30 minutes before you want to serve it. Use a spatula to remove it from the pan and parchment paper and carefully slide it onto a serving plate. Pile the cherries on top.

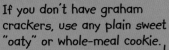

87

Top Tip

Make this a lighter treat by using a low-fat cream cheese and replace the heavy cream with low-fat sour cream.

Make sure you use the pitted cherries for the topping.

For a professional finish, slice the cheesecake before topping with the cherries.

Fruity variations

If you prefer, you can replace the cherries with other canned fruits, such as blueberries, or instead top your cheesecake with fresh fruit, such as sliced kiwifruit, strawberries, or bananas.

Drink up!

Feeling thirsty? Then look no further than this yummy assortment of thirst-quenching drinks. Whether you fancy something cool and fruity for a hot summer's day, or a warming winter hot chocolate, there is something for everyone here, so get guzzling!

Homemade lemonade (serves 4)

Pare the zest from 4 lemons, leaving the white pith behind, and place in a bowl with 3 cups boiling water and ½ cup superfine sugar. Put to one side for a few hours until cool. Remove the strips of zest and add the squeezed juice from the lemons. Ladle into glasses with a handful of ice cubes. If the flavor is too sharp, dilute with chilled carbonated water for a refreshing treat.

Strawberry and banana smoothie (serves 2)

Spoon 1¼ cups plain yogurt into a blender. Add about 9 oz (250 g) strawberries, 1 chopped banana, and 1 tbsp clear honey. Blend until smooth, then pour into glasses. For a chilled smoothie, add some ice. To invent your own smoothies, add your favorite fruit to the basic yogurt and banana mix.

For a healthier milk shake, use low-fat yogurt.

Berry milk shake (serves 2)

Place 1 sliced banana in a blender with ½ cup raspberries and ½ cup blueberries. Add 1 cup chilled milk, and ⅔ cup of strawberry or cherry yogurt. Blend together well, then pour into 2 tall glasses and top with extra fruit.

Nonalcoholic sangria (serves 6)

This classic drink is found all around Spain, with many different regional variations. This recipe uses grape juice instead of red wine. Pour 4¼ cups chilled grape juice into a large pitcher, and add the freshly squeezed juice from 2 oranges and 2 lemons. Top with 1 cup chilled lemon-flavored soda and add some sliced oranges and lemons. Serve each with a sprig of mint, a slice of lemon, and lots of ice.

Add different fruit, such as sliced apples and halved strawberries, to the sangria for a fruitier punch.

Sweet lassi (serves 4)

This cooling yogurt drink is popular all over India and Pakistan. To make it yourself, put 1¾ cups plain yogurt in a pitcher and stir in about 7 fl oz (200 ml) chilled water and 2 tsp sugar. Put some crushed ice in 4 tall glasses and pour over the lassi mixture. If you like, add some crushed cardamom seeds.

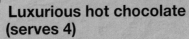

Luxurious hot chocolate (serves 4)

Pour 2½ cups milk into a saucepan followed by 3½ oz (100 g) dark chocolate. Cook over medium heat, stirring constantly, until the chocolate has melted. Bring the mixture to the boil, then whisk in 2–3 tbsp heavy cream until frothy. Test for sweetness, add sugar to taste, then pour into mugs.

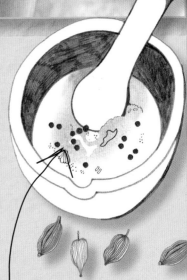

Crush cardamom seeds in a mortar and pestle.

Bake-off

Baking is like magic. You mix together a few ordinary-looking ingredients, put them in the oven, and they turn into something extraordinarily delicious—a soft, chewy loaf of bread, a crisp, cheesy pizza, or a sweet, crumbly pastry that melts in the mouth. Mmm.

Dinner rolls

Bread is easy and cheap to buy, so why bake your own? Simple, because there is nothing quite like the smell and taste of just-baked bread, still warm from the oven. But it's also a lot of fun to make, as you mix and shape the stretchy dough and see it rise.

Top Tip

For quick rolls, look out for instant dry yeast. Read the instructions on the package. Instant yeast is usually added straight to the flour, at the end of step 1. After step 2, go straight to step 5, kneading the dough for 10 minutes before shaping, rising, and baking.

MAKES 12 ROLLS
PREPARATION: 20 MINUTES,
 PLUS RISING
COOKING: 15–20 MINUTES

1 x ¼ oz (7 g) package
  dry yeast
1¾ cups warm water
6 cups white bread flour
1 tsp salt
1 tsp sugar
1 tbsp butter
extra flour, for dusting
olive oil, for greasing

1 Sprinkle the yeast over the water in a pitcher and set aside for 10 minutes, or until it starts to froth. Mix the flour, salt, and sugar together in a bowl, then rub in the butter with your fingers.

2 Add the water and yeast to the flour mixture and combine with your fingertips, until it forms a soft dough. If it's a little sticky, add some more flour.

3 Bring the dough together into a ball and knead on a floured work surface for 10 minutes. Use the heel of your hand to squash it away from you. Fold over the top, turn, and repeat until you have a smooth and elastic dough.

4 Place the dough in an oiled bowl, cover with oiled plastic wrap and a cloth and set aside for 30–40 minutes until the dough has doubled in size.

For a loaf, shape the dough into a large ball at step 5 and place in an oiled 2-lb (900-g) loaf pan Leave to rise then bake for 30–40 minutes.

5 Punch down the dough and knead it again for 5 minutes. Divide it into 12 pieces and shape each into a roll. Place them on a cookie sheet lined with parchment paper. Cover with oiled plastic wrap, and leave for 1 hour, or until doubled in size. Then preheat the oven to 425°F (220°C).

6 Sprinkle some flour over the rolls, then bake for 15–20 minutes until golden. You can tell if the rolls are cooked by tapping the bases—if they sound hollow, they're done, if not, put back in the oven for a few minutes.

For some decoration, sprinkle the rolls with a few sunflower or sesame seeds before baking.

Design a dough

Why not experiment and add some different flavors to your rolls? Mix in some chopped fresh herbs, garlic, olives, or even sun-dried tomatoes in step 2, for Mediterranean-style rolls.

Homemade pizza

Instead of ordering a pizza, why not make your own? Just adapt the recipe for bread dough to make the crusts, then pile them with toppings! Try one of these classic Italian recipes or create your own with your favorite ingredients.

Always tear basil. Chopping turns the leaves black, and they will release less flavor.

Pizza crust (makes 4)

Follow the recipe for bread dough (see pages 92–93), but use 2 tbsp olive oil instead of butter. Divide the dough into 4 balls. Preheat the oven to 425°F (220°C) . Roll each ball out into a 10-in (25-cm) pizza crust and place each on a greased cookie sheet. Spread each crust with a thin layer of passata and then your toppings. Season with salt and freshly ground black pepper, then cook in the oven for 10–12 minutes until crisp.

Fiorentina

Divide ¾ cup cooked, drained, and chopped spinach, ¼ tsp grated nutmeg, 1 tsp dried thyme, and 9 oz (250 g) sliced mozzarella cheese between the 4 pizza crusts. Crack an egg in the middle of each and sprinkle with some freshly grated Parmesan cheese.

Margherita

Divide 9 oz (250 g) sliced mozzarella cheese across the 4 pizza crusts. Scatter each with torn fresh basil leaves. Garnish with more basil after cooking.

Capricciosa

Divide between the 4 pizza crusts 9 oz (250 g) sliced mozzarella cheese, 8 sliced artichoke hearts, 4 sliced tomatoes, 4 thinly sliced mushrooms, 4 oz (115 g) chopped ham, and 4 tbsp pitted black olives.

You can buy artichoke hearts in a can, or in a jar, marinated in herbs, garlic, and oil.

You can swap Gorgonzola with Roquefort and ricotta with a soft goat cheese.

Roquefort

goat cheese

Quattro formaggi

Over the 4 pizza crusts, divide 4½ oz (125 g) mozzarella, ¼ cup freshly grated Parmesan, 4½ oz (125 g) Gorgonzola, and ½ cup ricotta. Sprinkle each with a pinch of dried oregano.

Calzone

Make any pizza into a calzone (folded pizza) by keeping the topping away from the edges. Then brush the rim with beaten egg and fold over each crust to enclose the filling, pressing the edges together with your fingers. Brush with olive oil, then bake in a preheated oven for 15–20 minutes.

Use a fork to crimp the edges.

Lemon pie

This classic dessert often features on the menus of top restaurants, but it's easy to make yourself at home. The rich, buttery base and silky-smooth fresh filling make a winning combination.

SERVES 8
PREPARATION: 25 MINUTES
COOKING: 50–60 MINUTES,
   PLUS CHILLING

For the pie crust
3 cups all-purpose
  flour, plus extra for dusting
1½ sticks butter, chilled
  and cubed
⅓ cup superfine sugar
2 eggs, beaten

For the filling
5 eggs
¾ cups superfine sugar
4 unwaxed lemons, zest and
  ⅔ cup squeezed juice
1 cup heavy cream

1 Sift the flour into a large bowl. Rub in the butter using your fingertips until the mixture looks like crumbs.

2 Stir in the sugar and beaten eggs. Then use your fingertips to bring all of the ingredients together into a soft ball of dough. Cover the dough in plastic wrap and chill in the refrigerator for 30 minutes.

3 Preheat the oven to 400°F (200°C). Lightly dust the work surface and a rolling pin with flour. Gently roll out the dough into a large thin circle, turning the dough clockwise every few rolls. If it starts to stick, dust with extra flour.

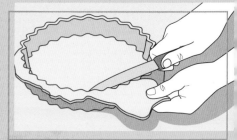

4 Carefully press the dough into a 9-in (23-cm) loose-bottom pie pan, and trim any excess with a knife. Line the pie shell with parchment paper, fill with baking beans or rice, and "bake blind" for 20 minutes (see page 121).

5 When you remove the pan from the oven, turn down the heat to 275°F (140°C). For the filling, whisk the eggs and sugar until combined. Stir in the lemon zest, lemon juice, and then the cream. Pour into the pie shell and bake for 30–40 minutes.

6 Allow the pie to cool and set for at least 30 minutes before slicing and serving.

Shortcut crust

Homemade dough is best, but you can cheat by buying a package of rolled pie crust, which you can press into the pan at step 4. Or, you can buy a ready-made cooked pie shell and then fill it in step 5.

For a finishing touch, dust the pie with confectioners' sugar and sprinkle over a little extra lemon zest.

Lemon pie is delicious served with cream and fresh berries.

Empanadas

These tasty stuffed pastries are found across Spain, Portugal, and South America, and each region has its own version. Once you know the basic method, you can try different fillings.

Top Tip
Add ½ tsp ground cumin and ½ tsp sweet paprika to the mixture at step 4 for a spicy twist.

MAKES 24
PREPARATION: 30 MINUTES,
** PLUS CHILLING**
COOKING: 25–30 MINUTES

For the pastry

4 cups all-purpose flour,
  plus extra for dusting
2 tsp baking powder
¾ stick butter, chilled
  and diced
2 eggs, beaten, plus extra
  to glaze
4–6 tbsp water

For the filling

1 tbsp olive oil
1 onion, finely chopped
4 tomatoes (about
  6 oz (175 g), chopped
2 tbsp tomato paste
¼ tsp dried chili flakes
  or powder
7 oz (200 g) can tuna, drained
2 tbsp finely chopped
  fresh parsley
salt and freshly
  ground black pepper

1 Sift the flour and baking powder into a large bowl. Rub in the butter with your fingertips until it looks like coarse breadcrumbs.

2 Add the beaten eggs and the water, a little at a time, mixing them in with a knife, then your fingertips, until a ball of dough is formed. Cover the pastry in plastic wrap and chill for 30 minutes.

3 Heat the oil in a frying pan and cook the onion over medium heat for 5–8 minutes, or until soft.

4 Add the tomatoes, tomato paste, chili flakes, tuna, and parsley, and season with salt and freshly ground black pepper. Reduce the heat and cook for 5–6 minutes, stirring occasionally. Set the mixture aside to cool.

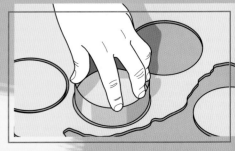

5 Preheat the oven to 375°F (190°C). Roll out the pastry on a floured surface to ⅛ in (3 mm) thick. Use a 3½-in (9-cm) cookie cutter to cut out circles. If you don't have a cookie cutter, you can use a clean can or cup to stamp out circles instead.

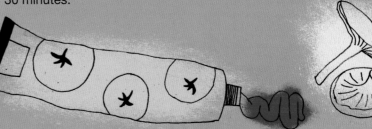

6 Put a heaped teaspoon of the filling inside each circle, then brush the edges with water. Fold the pastry over to form a half-moon shape, then firmly crimp the edges to seal.

7 Place the empanadas on a cookie sheet lined with parchment paper, and brush the tops with beaten egg. Bake for 25–30 minutes, or until golden brown. Serve warm.

These pastry packages make great picnic food.

Favorite fillings

You can replace the tuna with lots of different fillings. Brown 1 cup loose-packed ground beef in the pan after step 3. Or for a vegetarian version, add 9 oz (250 g) chopped mushrooms and 1 finely chopped garlic clove instead. Cook until any moisture has evaporated, then continue as above.

Puff-pastry tricks

Puff pastry is made up of many buttery layers that "puff" up when cooked. It's light, crispy, and delicious but tricky and time-consuming to make. The good news is that you can buy it already prepared, chilled or frozen. Sometimes the pastry is rolled out into a sheet, but it also comes in blocks. There are lots of ways to use it to make quick sweet and salty treats.

For a touch of spice before cooking, dust a little hot paprika over the beaten egg.

Cheese straws
Preheat the oven to 400°F (200°C). Roll out puff pastry to a rectangle about 0.25 in (0.5 cm) thick. Over half, scatter ½ cup grated cheese. Fold over the plain half and roll out again to a rectangle 0.25 in (0.5 cm) thick. Brush with beaten egg and sprinkle with grated Parmesan cheese. Cut into 0.5-in (1-cm) strips, twist each strip several times, and place on a cookie sheet. Bake for 12 minutes, or until golden.

Tomato and olive pie
Preheat the oven to 425°F (220°C). Place a rectangle of puff pastry about 0.25 in (0.5 cm) thick on to a greased cookie sheet. Using a knife, score a border 1 in (2.5 cm) from the edges, being careful not to cut all the way through. Spread the center with 2 tbsp black olive paste and 1 tbsp pesto (see page 61) and cover with slices of tomato and pitted black olives. Brush the border with beaten egg and bake for 20–25 minutes. Scatter with basil leaves to serve.

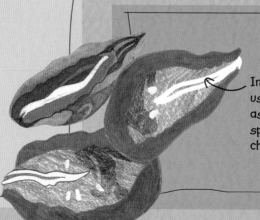

Invent your own pies using ingredients such as sun-dried tomatoes, spinach, anchovies, feta cheese, and red onion.

Sausage rolls

Preheat the oven to 400°F (200°C). Roll the puff pastry to a 8-in (20-cm) square 0.25 in (0.5 cm) thick, and cut it in half to get two strips. Spread 2 tsp prepared mustard down the middle of each strip. Cut the skins from 1 lb (450 g) sausages and place them in a line on the mustard. Dampen the edge of the pastry with water, fold over, and press the edges together. Cut each half into 8–10 pieces. Brush with beaten egg and cut slits in the top. Bake on a greased cookie sheet for 20–25 minutes, or until golden.

You can wrap some herbs or lightly fried onion inside the pastry along with the sausage.

Apple strudel

Preheat the oven to 400°F (200°C). Mix together 3 peeled, cored, and thinly sliced apples, ½ cup light brown sugar, 1 tsp ground cinnamon, ½ cup golden raisins, and the zest of 1 orange. Place a rectangle of puff pastry onto a lined cookie sheet. Place the filling down one side and fold the other side of the pastry over, sealing the edges with a little water. Turn the strudel over so that the sealed edge is underneath, brush with beaten egg, and bake for 35–40 minutes, or until golden. Sprinkle with confectioners' sugar.

If you like nuts, add ½ cup chopped walnuts or pecans to the filling.

Try sprinkling a little ground cinnamon or nutmeg over the pastry before you roll it up.

Palmiers

Preheat the oven to 400°F (200°C). Roll out the puff pastry to a rectangle about 10 x 12 in (25 x 30 cm) on a sugared surface. Brush with melted butter and sprinkle with ¼ cup granulated sugar. Roll up one long edge into the middle, then roll in the other edge and press them together. Chill for 30 minutes, then cut into 0.5-in (1-cm) slices and place them on a lined cookie sheet. Bake for 12–15 minutes, or until golden.

Chocolate cake

Treat yourself with this rich and fudgy cake topped with a sticky chocolate frosting. The cake will actually taste better if you make it a few days before you want to serve it, but it's so delicious that it might not last that long!

SERVES 8
PREPARATION: 30 MINUTES
COOKING: 35–40 MINUTES

For the cake

6 oz (175 g) dark chocolate
1 stick butter, cubed,
 plus extra for greasing
½ tsp vanilla extract
⅓ cup superfine sugar
3 eggs, separated
⅓ cup self-rising flour
¾ cup ground almonds

For the frosting

4 oz (115 g) dark chocolate
⅔ cup heavy cream
2 oz (60 g) milk chocolate for
 chocolate curls (optional)

For a very rich cake, use dark chocolate with at least 60 percent cocoa solids.

1 Preheat the oven to 375°F (190°C). Lightly grease and line the base of a deep 8-in (20-cm) cake pan with butter and parchment paper.

2 Break the chocolate into pieces and place in a heatproof bowl above a saucepan of simmering water. Stir until all of the chocolate has melted. Add the butter and vanilla extract, and stir until the butter has melted and all of the ingredients are combined.

3 Put the sugar and egg yolk in a large bowl and whisk together until thick, pale, and creamy.

4 Stir the chocolate mixture into the eggs and sugar, sift in the flour, and fold in the ground almonds. Mix until all of the ingredients are well combined.

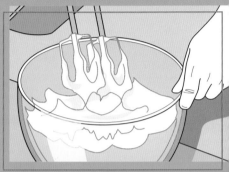

5 Whisk the egg whites in a large bowl until they form stiff peaks. Stir half into the chocolate mixture until smooth and well combined, then gently fold in the rest.

6 Pour the cake mixture into the pan and bake for 35–40 minutes. Cool in the pan for 5 minutes, then turn the cake out onto a wire rack to cool completely.

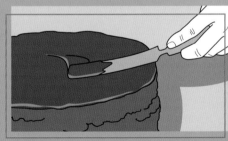

7 To make the frosting, melt the chocolate and heavy cream in a saucepan over gentle heat, stirring often until it forms a smooth, silky paste. Pour onto the cooled cake and smooth over the top and sides with a spatula. Decorate with grated milk chocolate or chocolate curls (see opposite).

Top Tip

To make chocolate curls, use a potato peeler to slowly shave the sides of a chocolate bar. Make sure the chocolate is at room temperature—if it's too warm or cold, the curls won't form.

A touch of orange

Chocolate and orange is a classic combination, so why not spice up your cake by adding the zest of 1 orange to the cake mixture in step 4—or use orange-flavored chocolate.

Brownies

When only something chocolaty will do, these fudgy brownies are just what you need. They make a delicious dessert eaten warm with ice cream, but they are also great on their own.

MAKES 12 BROWNIES
PREPARATION: 20 MINUTES
COOKING: 20–25 MINUTES

1 stick unsalted butter,
  softened to room temperature
7 oz (200 g) dark chocolate
1 cup plus 2 tbsp
  superfine sugar
1 tsp vanilla extract
4 large eggs, beaten
½ cup plus 1 tbsp
  all-purpose flour
½ cup cocoa powder

1 Preheat the oven to 350°F (180°C). Grease and line a rectangular cake pan (about 6 x 10 in/15 x 25 cm) with a little of the butter and parchment paper.

2 Break the chocolate into pieces and place in a heatproof bowl. Rest the bowl over a saucepan of simmering water for a few minutes, stirring until the chocolate has melted.

3 Beat together the remaining butter, the sugar, and vanilla extract with a wooden spoon, balloon or electric whisk until pale and fluffy. Beat in the eggs, a little at a time, until they have all been added and the mixture is smooth and creamy.

4 Sift in the flour and cocoa, a bit at a time, while stirring the mixture. Pour in the melted chocolate and mix everything together well.

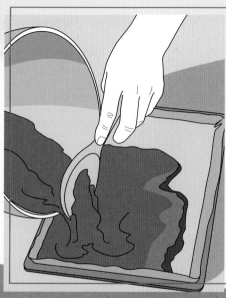

5 Spoon the mixture into the prepared cake pan and bake for 20–25 minutes. It should be crisp on top but still slightly gooey inside. Leave to cool in the pan for about 10 minutes. Then transfer the brownie in its paper onto a wire rack to cool a little more before cutting it into squares.

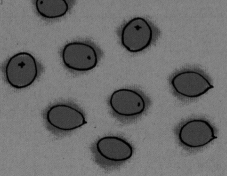

Top Tip
Poke a skewer in the middle of the brownie to test if it is cooked. If it comes out slightly wet, it's ready! If it still looks like cake batter, put it back in the oven for a few minutes.

Serve warm with ice cream and fresh raspberries for a really yummy dessert.

Go fruit and nuts!
Add some chopped nuts such as pecans, filberts, or Brazil nuts to your brownie mixture before baking. Alternatively, try some dried sour cherries, cranberries, or the grated zest of an orange.

Blueberry muffins

There are countless different muffin flavors, but blueberry is a classic. Light, fluffy, and bursting with berries, these are delicious eaten warm from the oven and are definitely best on the day they are baked.

MAKES 12 MUFFINS
PREPARATION: 20 MINUTES
COOKING: 20–25 MINUTES

2¼ cups all-purpose flour
½ cup ground almonds
1 tbsp baking powder
⅓ cup superfine sugar
1 cup milk
3 eggs, beaten
1 stick unsalted
  butter, melted
2 lemons, zest only
1½ cups fresh blueberries

1 Preheat the oven to 400°F (200°C). Line a 12-cup muffin pan with paper muffin cups.

2 Sift the flour, almonds, baking powder, and sugar into a large bowl and mix them together. In a separate bowl, whisk together the milk, eggs, melted butter, and lemon zest.

3 Pour the whisked egg mixture into the dry mixture and gently mix them together. Don't overmix—it doesn't matter if the batter is lumpy. The less mixing you do, the lighter the muffins will be. Stir in the blueberries.

4 Spoon the mixture into the muffin cups, then bake in the preheated oven for 20–25 minutes, or until the tops are golden and firm to touch. Cool in the pan for 5 minutes before transferring to a wire rack to cool completely.

Top Tip
As you add the blueberries, squash them between your thumb and finger so the juice will run out in beautiful purple ripples as the muffins bake.

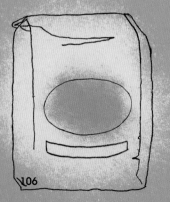

For a crunchy top, scatter over a few slivered almonds and a little sugar before baking.

Mix 'n' match mixture

If you like some chocolate in your muffins, add 2½ oz (75 g) white chocolate chunks to the mixture with the blueberries. You can also swap the blueberries for chopped strawberries or diced peaches.

Decorate the cake with a little orange zest or some whole nuts.

Flour power
Use whole-wheat self-rising flour instead of white flour if you like— it will give the cake a nice nutty flavor.

Carrot cake

Putting carrots in a cake might sound strange, but don't knock it until you've tried it! They make the cake deliciously moist and sweet. This version also has a hint of spice and is topped with a tangy cream-cheese frosting.

SERVES 8
PREPARATION: 25 MINUTES
COOKING: 25–30 MINUTES

For the cake

1¼ cups self-rising flour

2 tsp baking powder

2 tsp ground cinnamon

1 tsp ground ginger

¾ cups light brown sugar

½ cup chopped
pecans or walnuts

⅓ cup raisins

5 oz (140 g) carrots, peeled
and grated

⅔ cup sunflower oil,
plus extra for greasing

2 large eggs, beaten

2 tbsp fresh orange juice

For the frosting

1¼ cups full fat
cream cheese

1 cup confectioners' sugar

1 orange, zest and
2 tbsp juice

1 Preheat the oven to 350°F (180°C) and grease and line the bases of two 8-in (20-cm) round cake pans with a little oil and parchment paper.

2 Mix the flour, baking powder, spices, and sugar in a bowl. Add the nuts, raisins, and carrots and then stir to mix everything together.

3 In a separate bowl, whisk together the oil, eggs, and orange juice, then fold into the dry ingredients.

4 Divide the mixture between the pans and bake for 25–30 minutes, or until risen and springy to touch. Leave to rest in the pans for 10 minutes, then turn out onto a wire rack to cool.

5 Beat together the cream cheese, confectioners' sugar, orange zest, and juice until smooth. Sandwich the cakes with one third of the frosting and spread the rest over the top and sides with a spatula.

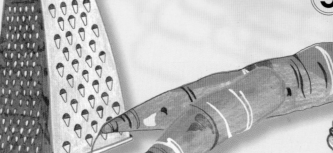

109

Cool cupcakes

Cupcakes are the trendiest treats around. Decorated with exquisite frostings and toppings, they often look too good to eat! Make your own with this simple vanilla cupcake recipe and four fun variations. Always stick to the quantities of basic ingredients in the cake mixture, but you can get creative with fun flavors and decorations. All recipes make 12 cakes.

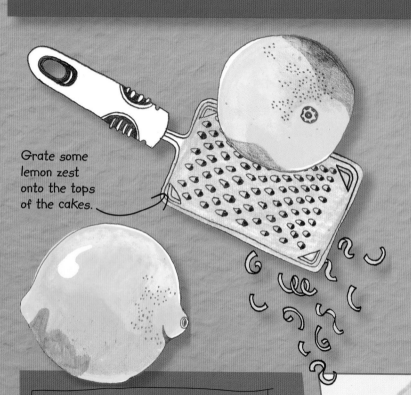

Grate some lemon zest onto the tops of the cakes.

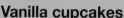

Vanilla cupcakes
Preheat the oven to 375°F (190°C). Line a 12-cup muffin pan with paper muffin cups. Beat 1 stick butter and ½ cup superfine sugar in a bowl until pale and fluffy. Beat in 2 eggs and ½ tsp vanilla extract then fold in 1 cup self-rising flour. Divide between the paper cups. Bake for 15–20 minutes until golden. For the frosting, beat 1 cup confectioners' sugar with ¾ stick softened unsalted butter, ½ tsp vanilla extract, and 1 tbsp milk until creamy. Spread on the cakes and decorate.

Lemon cupcakes
Replace the vanilla extract in the cake mixture with the zest of 2 lemons. Bake as before. While the cakes are in the oven, mix ⅓ cup confectioners' sugar with the juice of ½ a lemon to make a syrup. While the cakes are still warm, make a few holes in the tops with a skewer. Spoon 1 tsp syrup over each cake. Omit the vanilla and milk from the frosting mixture and replace with 1 tbsp lemon juice. When the cakes are cool, spread over the frosting.

Banana and maple cupcakes

Mash 1 ripe banana and stir into the cake mixture with an extra ¼ cup self-rising flour and ⅓ cup chopped pecans. Bake as before. For the frosting, replace the vanilla and 3 tbsp of the confectioners' sugar with 2 tbsp maple syrup. When the cakes are cool, spread over the frosting.

Top with sliced strawberries and confectioners' sugar.

Strawberry cheesecake cupcakes

Divide 12 chopped strawberries between the muffin cups. Spoon the cake mixture on top and bake as before. For the frosting, beat 1 cup confectioners' sugar and ½ tsp vanilla extract into 2 tbsp softened unsalted butter and ¼ cup full fat cream cheese until smooth. When the cakes are cool, slice off the top of each one, spoon on some of the frosting, and then put the tops back on.

Sprinkles or small candies are a great way to quickly decorate cupcakes.

Chocolate cupcakes

Replace ¼ cup of the flour in the cake mixture with the same amount of sifted cocoa powder. Divide between the muffin cups, then bake as before. For chocolate frosting, add 2 tbsp cocoa powder to the vanilla frosting with an extra 1 tbsp milk. Whisk in 2 oz (60 g) melted and cooled dark chocolate. When the cakes are cool, spread over the frosting. Decorate with chocolate sprinkles, chocolate chips, or grated chocolate.

Choc-chip cookies

No one turns down a homemade choc-chip cookie, especially when it's still warm from the oven and gooey inside. You can make these cookies with ready-made choc chips but, even better, is to take a bar of chocolate and chop it into big chunks.

MAKES 12–15 COOKIES
PREPARATION: 20 MINUTES
COOKING: 10–15 MINUTES

1 stick plus 1 tbsp
  unsalted butter
¾ cup light brown sugar
1 egg
2 tsp vanilla extract
1¾ cups all-purpose flour
½ tsp baking powder
3½ oz (100 g) milk chocolate
  chopped into chunks

1 Preheat the oven to 375°F (190°C). Line 2 large cookie sheets with parchment paper. Melt the butter in a saucepan over gentle heat.

2 Put the sugar into a large mixing bowl, pour over the melted butter, and beat with a wooden spoon.

3 Beat the egg into the mixture with the vanilla extract until everything is blended together.

4 Sift the flour and baking powder into the mixture, a little at a time, and stir in. Then add the chocolate chunks. Don't worry if it looks sticky.

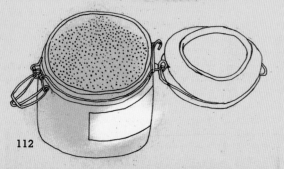

5 Drop heaped spoonfuls of the mixture onto the cookie sheets. Slightly flatten the tops and leave plenty of space between them. Bake in the oven for 10–12 minutes, or until just turning golden brown. Leave to cool down a little on the sheets. Then use a spatula to transfer the cookies to a wire rack to cool and harden some more before digging in.

Top Tip
If you don't eat all of the cookies right away, store them in an airtight container to eat the next day. You'll find that they get extra chewy overnight.

Try nuts, candied orange peel, or even dried fruit in your cookie dough.

Cookie sandwich

If you like choc-chip cookies and ice cream, why not be greedy and combine the two? For a truly delicious treat, sandwich two cookies together with a scoop of chocolate or vanilla ice cream.

Macaroons

Crisp on the outside and nice and chewy on the inside, these almondy treats are surprisingly easy to make, so why not whip up a batch for your friends?

Top Tip
Store the macaroons in an airtight container as soon as they have cooled. They will go soft, however, so eat them up quickly!

MAKES 12 MACAROONS
PREPARATION: 10–15 MINUTES,
 PLUS RESTING
COOKING: 25–30 MINUTES

1 cup ground almonds
7 oz (200 g) confectioners' sugar
2 large egg whites
½ tsp cream of tartar
2 tbsp superfine sugar
a few drops of almond extract
12 whole blanched almonds

1 Line a cookie sheet with parchment paper. Mix together the ground almonds and the confectioners' sugar in a bowl.

2 Whisk the egg whites until they form stiff peaks, then whisk in the cream of tartar and superfine sugar until glossy. Gently fold in the almond extract and the ground almond and confectioners' sugar mixture.

3 Place 12 spoonfuls of the mixture onto the lined sheets and smooth out with a damp finger to form circles about ½ in (1 cm) thick. Leave enough space between them to allow for spreading.

4 Place 1 almond on each spoonful of mixture and set aside for 30 minutes, or until the outsides are no longer sticky.

5 Preheat the oven to 300°F (150°C). Bake for 25–30 minutes, or until tinged with brown. Leave to cool for 5 minutes and then carefully peel away the parchment paper. Cool completely on a wire rack.

You can drizzle the cooled macaroons with some melted dark chocolate.

Ginger cookies

These spicy cookies smell wonderful when baking in the oven. It's fun to make them into shapes such as stars or even people, but simple circles taste just as good!

Top Tip
If you like very gingery cookies, add another teaspoon of ground ginger to the dough.

MAKES 30
PREPARATION: 20–25 MINUTES
COOKING: 10–12 MINUTES

3 cups all-purpose flour, plus
  extra for dusting
1 tsp baking soda
2 tsp ground ginger
1 stick butter, plus extra
  for greasing
¾ cup light brown sugar
4 tbsp light corn syrup
1 egg, beaten

1 Preheat the oven to 375°F (190°C) and line 3 cookie sheets with parchment paper. Place the flour, baking soda, and ginger into a bowl. Add the butter and use your fingertips to rub it in to the flour until it resembles fine bread crumbs.

2 Stir in the sugar. Add the corn syrup and beaten egg and mix to form a smooth dough, using your hands to bring the mixture together and knead it lightly.

3 Cut the dough in half and roll out one half on a lightly floured work surface until about ¼ in (5 mm) thick. Use a 2¾-in (7-cm) cookie cutter to cut out circles. Place them on the lined sheets, using a spatula.

4 Repeat with the remaining dough, then bake the cookies in batches in the oven for 10–12 minutes or until they are a darkish shade of brown. Allow to cool a bit on the sheets then use a spatula to remove them to a wire rack to cool completely.

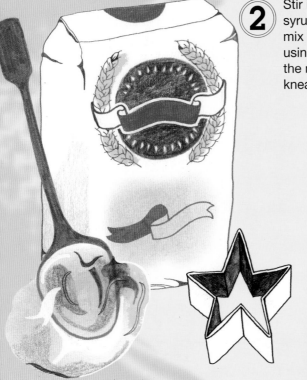

115

Back to basics

There are a few techniques, tips, and tricks that, once you know them, make cooking much easier. This section shows you what you need to know. There's also a guide to the most popular herbs and spices and a glossary to some cooking terms to help you on your way.

Tricks and tips

A little know-how can help you achieve the best results and prevent problems in the kitchen. This step-by-step guide shows you some useful techniques that will make cooking easier.

CHOPPING AN ONION

1. Peel the onion, cut it in half, and lay the cut side down. Make a few horizontal slices, cutting up to, but not through, the root.

2. Firmly hold the root end of the onion, then slice down vertically through the layers, from the top of the onion to the root.

PEELING A TOMATO

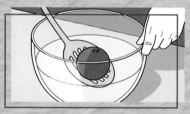

1. Put the tomato in a bowl and pour over boiling water. Leave for 10–20 seconds, then transfer to a bowl of cold water using a slotted spoon.

2. When the tomato is cool enough to handle, peel off its loosened skin with a knife.

CHOPPING GARLIC

1. Slice off the root end of the garlic clove, then loosen the peel by placing the flat side of a knife on top and pressing down firmly.

2. Remove the skin, then slice down through the clove into thin pieces. For finely chopped garlic, cut across the slices.

PREPARING A CHILI

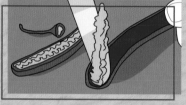

1. Use a small sharp knife to cut off the stalk, then halve the chilli lengthwise. Use the tip of the knife to scrape out the seeds.

2. Slice the chili lengthwise into strips, then hold the strips together in a bundle and slice across to get tiny cubes.

Watch out!
The ingredient in chilies that gives them their heat can sting your eyes and skin. Never rub your eyes or nose when handling chilies, and wash your hands and utensils well once you have finished preparing them.

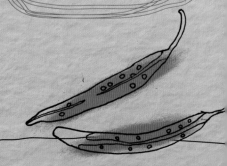

PREPARING DRIED LEGUMES

1. Soak legumes, such as lentils and beans, overnight in cold water until they have become swollen. The bigger the legume, the longer it takes to soak.

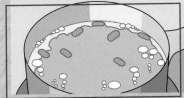

2. Cooking time varies between legumes, and can take between 45 minutes and a few hours. Add a pinch of salt toward the end of cooking time.

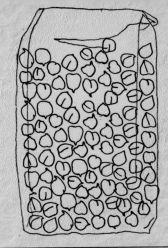

COOKING RICE

1. Allow 2½ oz (75 g) per person. Rinse the rice in a strainer under cold running water, then put it into a large saucepan.

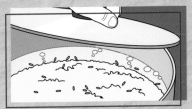

2. Cook the rice in double its quantity of water. Bring to the boil, stir, then lower the heat and simmer for the time given on the package.

3. Drain well, return to the pan, cover, and leave for 5 minutes. Just before serving, fluff up the rice with a fork to separate the grains.

COOKING DRIED EGG NOODLES

1. Bring a pan of water to the boil. Add the noodles, then bring the water back to the boil. Turn off the heat, cover, and leave for 5 minutes.

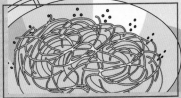

2. Drain in a colander and serve. If you are not eating the noodles immediately, run under cold water, drain, and toss them in a little oil to prevent sticking.

BOILING DRIED PASTA

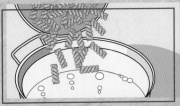

1. Bring a large pan of salted water to the boil. Add the pasta and stir. Boil, uncovered, for the time recommended time on the package.

MARINATING

1. Using a sharp knife, make shallow cuts into the meat or fish that you are marinating, to allow the flavors to seep in.

2. In a nonmetallic dish, mix the food and marinade until well coated. Leave for a minimum of 30 minutes. Meat can be left overnight in the fridge.

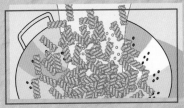

2. Drain the pasta using a colander, gently shaking it to remove any excess water.

Baking techniques

Take the heat out of baking by getting to grips with these basic techniques and terms. Once you know how things are done, you'll find baking a breeze.

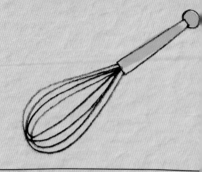

RUBBING IN

1. Chop cold butter into small pieces with a knife, then add them to the flour in a large mixing bowl.

2. Take a small quantity of the butter and flour and rub it between your thumbs and fingertips to mix, letting it fall back into the bowl.

3. Continue rubbing in until there are no big lumps of butter left and the mixture looks like fine bread crumbs.

FOLDING IN

This is a method of gentle stirring to keep as much air in the mixture as possible. Use a spatula to cut through and turn the ingredients until mixed.

ROLLING OUT PASTRY

1. Sprinkle a little flour onto the work surface and the rolling pin to prevent them from sticking.

2. Gently roll the pastry away from you, then carefully turn it and sprinkle with flour if it sticks. Roll and rotate until you get the right shape.

PREPARING A CAKE PAN

1. Place the cake pan on a piece of parchment paper and trace around the base. Cut the shape out just inside the traced line.

2. Use a pastry brush to coat the bottom and sides of the cake pan with a thin layer of melted butter.

3. Put the paper into the cake pan. The melted butter will hold it in place.

BAKING PASTRY BLIND

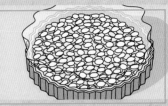

1. Press the rolled-out pastry into the pan and trim any excess. Prick the base with a fork, then chill for 30 minutes. Line with a piece of parchment paper.

2. Fill with dried beans, or rice, then bake at 400°F (200°C) for 10 minutes. Remove the paper and beans, or rice, and cook for another 5 minutes.

To test if a cake is cooked, poke a skewer in the middle—if it comes out clean, it's ready.

KNEADING DOUGH

1. Use the heel of your hand to squash the dough away from you, then fold the far edge back over the top and turn the dough a quarter turn.

2. Repeat the pressing, folding, and turning action until you have smooth, silky, and elastic dough. This will take about 10 minutes.

PUNCHING DOWN DOUGH

To make sure bread has an even texture, the air is "punched down" from the risen dough. To do this, simply punch it gently with your fist.

SEPARATING AN EGG

1. Firmly tap the egg on the side of the bowl, insert the tips of your thumbs inside the crack, and pull apart, keeping the yolk in one half of the shell.

2. Gently tip the yolk from one half of the shell to the other, letting the egg white fall into the bowl. Put the yolk into a separate bowl.

WHIPPING CREAM

Gently whisk the cream until it thickens and forms soft peaks when the whisk is lifted. Be careful not to overwhip or the cream will start to separate.

WHISKING EGG WHITES

1. Put the egg whites into a clean, grease-free bowl. Whisk with an electric hand beater at medium speed for 1 minute.

2. Turn the speed to high and whisk until the egg whites increase in volume, forming stiff peaks. Do not overwhisk or the egg whites will break apart.

MELTING CHOCOLATE

Break the chocolate into a heatproof bowl and set over a pan of gently simmering water. Stir occasionally until melted.

Herbs

In cooking, herbs are the leaves of plants that are added to food. Woody herbs, like rosemary and bay leaves, have strong flavors and you add them to the dish as it cooks. Soft herbs, like basil and parsley, can be eaten raw and should be added just before serving.

Oregano goes really well with pasta and pizza.

Oregano

Cilantro

Italian parsley (left) has a slightly finer and stronger flavour than curly parsley (right).

Parsley

Cool, refreshing mint is good for serving alongside hot, spicy dishes.

Mint

There are hundreds of varieties of thyme, each with a slightly different aroma.

Dill is used a lot in fish dishes.

Dill

Thyme

Basil

Chives are the smallest member of the onion family.

The Greeks and Romans crowned their kings and Olympic champions with wreaths of bay leaves.

Bay leaves

Tarragon is great with chicken.

Tarragon

Chives

Rosemary

Fresh or dried?
Woody herbs keep their flavor when dried and are worth buying in jars for the pantry. Soft herbs, such as basil, parsley, mint, cilantro, and chives, don't taste like much when dried so try to use them fresh. Why not grow your own, either indoors or in the garden?

Spices

Spices are the roots, seeds, buds, fruits, and bark of tropical plants. Some milder spices are used whole, while the more powerful ones are used in ground form, so you can add a pinch or two to flavor your cooking.

Saffron is the dried stigmas of the saffron crocus, and is the most expensive spice in the world.

Cumin

Vanilla is used in baking as beans and as a liquid extract.

Saffron

Vanilla

Nutmeg

The ground bark of cinnamon is often used in cakes and cookies.

Coriander seed

Turmeric

Cardamom

Cinnamon

This is a strong spice made from red-hot chili peppers.

Cayenne pepper

Ginger is used fresh and dried.

Ginger

Cloves

Mustard seed

Chilies
The biggest spice crop in the world is chili peppers. There are hundreds of varieties, ranging from mild and slightly tingling to explosively hot. The hottest fresh chilies are usually the smallest ones with the thinnest skin.

Paprika is made from dried red bell peppers—it comes in different flavors, from hot to mildly sweet, and smoked.

Paprika

Black pepper

Glossary

Bain-marie
A pan of water in which you put another pan, containing food, to cook gently.

Bake blind
To cook an empty pie crust lined with paper and dried beans or rice (see page 121).

Baste
To spoon fat over food as it cooks to keep it moist and add flavor.

Batter
An uncooked mixture of flour and liquid, such as pancake batter.

Beat
To stir vigorously, usually with a wooden spoon.

Blend
To mix ingredients together with a spoon. Also, to use a blender to purée ingredients.

Brown
To cook food until it turns golden brown in color.

Caramelize
To heat sugar until it turns brown. Also a term used to describe the sugars in food, such as onions, turning brown when they are heated.

Carbohydrate
One of a group of foods that includes starchy and sugary foods used by the body to make energy.

Concentrate
A solution that is strong in flavor because some of the water in it has evaporated.

Cream
To mix together fat and sugar with a wooden spoon to incorporate air into the mixture.

Crimp
To fold or pinch together the edges of pastry or dough for decoration, or to seal in the filling.

Curdle
To cause milk or sauce to separate into solids and liquid.

Dash
A small amount of seasoning.

Deseed
To remove and discard the seeds from fruit or vegetables.

Dice
To cut food into small cubes.

Dollop
A large spoonful of food.

Drizzle
To trickle a very small amount of liquid or oil over food.

Dry-fry
To cook food in a frying pan without any added fat or oil.

Fiber
The part of plant food that is not digested and that passes through the digestive system and out of the body.

Fold
To combine ingredients, by cutting and mixing gently, so as to keep as much air in the mixture as possible (see page 120).

Glaze
To brush a mixture over food either to give it flavor or a glossy finish.

Grate
To rub food over a grater to give fine or coarse shreds.

Grill (indoor)
To cook food in a special ridged pan.

Hull
To remove the green leaves and coarse centers of soft fruit.

Knead
To stretch and fold dough until it becomes elastic and smooth (see page 121).

Marinade
A liquid that adds flavor and may tenderize food.

Marinate
To leave food in a marinade to flavor and tenderize it.

Mineral
A nutrient found in food that is essential in small amounts to keep the body healthy.

Parboil
To partially cook food in boiling water.

Pat
A small amount of fat—about one teaspoon.

Pinch
The amount of an ingredient that you can pick up between your thumb and index finger.

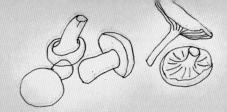

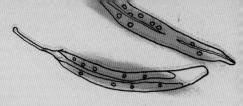

Poach
To cook food, such as fish or eggs, in a gently simmering liquid.

Protein
One of a group of foods, such as meat, eggs, legumes, nuts, and seeds, that includes ingredients that are essential for keeping your body strong.

Purée
Food that has been mashed, strained, crushed, or pulsed in a blender or food processor until smooth.

Punch down
To punch risen bread dough to return it to its original size before shaping (see page 121).

Reduce
To thicken and intensify the flavor of a liquid by boiling it uncovered so that the excess water evaporates.

Rest
To set food aside for a short time— for example, roasted meat is rested so that it becomes moist and tender.

Roast
To cook with a little fat in a baking pan in the oven.

Rub in
To rub together a flour and fat mixture between your fingers and thumbs until it resembles bread crumbs (see page 120).

Salmonella
A bacterium that can cause food poisoning.

Sauté
To fry food in a small amount of fat, frequently stirring it so that it browns evenly.

Score
To make shallow cuts over the surface of food.

Seal
To brown the surface of meat in a small amount of hot fat to lock in its juices.

Season
To add salt and pepper, according to taste, to improve or bring out the flavor in a dish.

Set
To leave a soft food to become firm.

Shallow-fry
To cook food in a small amount of fat or oil in a frying pan.

Shred
To tear or cut food into fine strips.

Simmer
To cook food so that it bubbles gently.

Stand
To put food to one side for a short period of time.

Stir-fry
To cook pieces of food in a small amount of very hot oil, usually in a wok, stirring constantly.

Stock
A liquid flavored with the meat, fish, or vegetables that were cooked in it, often used to make a soup or sauce. Stock can also be made by adding water to a stock cube or bouillon powder.

Strain
To pass food through a fine mesh strainer to remove lumps, add air, or produce a purée.

Syrup
A concentrated solution of sugar and water.

Toast
To cook food until it is golden brown, either under the broiler or in a pan.

Vitamin
One of the essential nutrients in food that your body needs in order to work properly and stay healthy.

Whip/whisk
To beat ingredients, such as cream or egg whites, to add air and make them thicker.

Zest
The thin colored outer layer of a citrus fruit, which contains flavor in its oils.

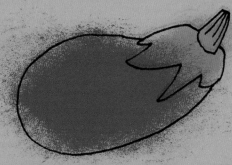

Index

Credits

Dorling Kindersley would like to thank:
Jessamy Wood for editorial help, Andrew Leeke for design assistance, Stephanie Pliakas for proofreading, Jackie Brind for preparing the index, and Carolyn Humphries for converting the recipes.

The publisher would like to thank the following for their kind permission to reproduce their images:

(Key: a-above; b-below/ bottom; c-centre; l-left; r-right; t-top)

Corbis: Riou / Photocuisine 101bc. **Dorling Kindersley:** Rough Guides 94cl. **Getty Images:** Foodcollection RF 13bc, 97; FoodPix / Alexandra Grablewski 31bl; Nordic Photos / Janne Hansson 93; Photodisc / Liza McCorkle 111bl; Photographer's Choice / Still Images 85; Photographer's Choice RF / Jamie Grill 64tr; StockFood Creative / Alain Caste 89bl; StockFood Creative / Chris Alack 55; StockFood Creative / Clare Plueckhahn 110tr; StockFood Creative / Ellen Silverman 37cl; StockFood Creative / Evan Sklar 77tl; StockFood Creative / Jorn Rynio 94crb; StockFood Creative / Leigh Beisch 95bl; StockFood Creative / Louise Lister 36tr, 76cl; StockFood Creative / Luzia Ellert 65cl; StockFood Creative / Marc O. Finley 77cl; StockFood Creative / Rita Maas 65bc; StockFood Creative / Sam Stowell 29; StockFood Creative / Ulrike Koeb 18br; UpperCut Images / MIB Pictures 30bl. **iStockphoto.com:** Steve Debenport 113; Giancarlo Polacchini 89tc; Rusm 18-19; travellinglight 45br.

Photolibrary: FoodCollection 21, 77br. **StockFood.com:** Chris Alack 101tc; Bayside 59; Uwe Bender 88br; Bialy, Dorota i Bogdan 14tr; Rua Castilho 23bl; Jean Cazals 65tr; Hannes Eichinger 70br; Eising 12br; Geoff Fenney 110br, 111tc; Foodfolio 71tr; Louise Hammond 77tr, 100cl; Lara Hata 71br; John Hay 44bl; Marie Jose Jarry 23tc; Dave King 61bl; Jo Kirchherr 70tr; Robbert Koene 74; Laurange 50; Studio Lipov 76tr; Renato Marcialis 101cl; Chugrad McAndrews 25; Gareth Morgans 37br; Karl Newedel 95tc; P. Nilsson 61cr; Stefan Oberschelp 64bl; William Reavell 35; Rob Fiocca Photography 82; J. Rynio 70cl; Bodo A. Schieren 95c; Sam Stowell 49; Teubner Foodfoto 40; Viennaslide / Richter 60cr; Frank Wieder 60cl; Tanya Zouev 111c.

Jacket images: Front: **Corbis:** Birgid Allig bl; Simon Marcus t. **Getty Images:** FoodPix / James and James br; StockFood Creative / Ulrike Koeb bc. iStockphoto.com: Wallace Price bc (staple), bl (staple), br (staple), fbl (staple), fbr (staple); Nic Taylor bc (instant film), bl (instant film), br (instant film), fbl (instant film), fbr (instant film). Back: **Alamy Images:** Imagebroker c. iStockphoto.com: Uyen Le (knife and fork). Spine: **iStockphoto. com:** Uyen Le.

All other images © Dorling Kindersley
For further information see:
www.dkimages.com